LIGUORI CATHOLIC ... STUDY

Universal Letters

JAMES, 1 AND 2 PETER,
1, 2, AND 3 JOHN,
JUDE

WILLIAM A. ANDERSON, DMIN, PHD

Liguori

LIGUORI, MISSOURI

Imprimi Potest:
Harry Grile, CSsR, Provincial
Denver Province, The Redemptorists

Printed with Ecclesiastical Permission and Approved for Private or Instructional Use

Nihil Obstat: Rev. Msgr. Kevin Michael Quirk, JCD, JV
              Censor Librorum

Imprimatur: + Michael J. Bransfield
             Bishop of Wheeling-Charleston [West Virginia]
             November 14, 2013

Published by Liguori Publications
Liguori, Missouri 63057

To order, call 800-325-9521
www.liguori.org

Cataloging-in-Publication Data is on file with the Library of Congress.

p ISBN 978-0-7648-2129-5
e ISBN 978-0-7648-6926-6

Liguori Publications, a nonprofit corporation, is an apostolate of The Redemptorists. To learn more about The Redemptorists, visit Redemptorists.com.

Printed in the United States of America
18 17 16 15 14 / 5 4 3 2 1
First Edition

Contents

NOTE: The length of each Bible section varies. Group leaders should combine sections as needed to fit the number of sessions in their program.

Dedication

THIS SERIES is lovingly dedicated to the memory of my parents, Angor and Kathleen Anderson, in gratitude for all they shared with all who knew them, especially my siblings and me.

Acknowledgments

BIBLE STUDIES and reflections depend on the help of others who read the manuscript and make suggestions. I am especially indebted to Sister Anne Francis Bartus, CSJ, DMin, whose vast experience and knowledge were very helpful in bringing this series to its final form.

Introduction to
Liguori Catholic Bible Study

READING THE BIBLE can be daunting. It's a complex book, and many a person of goodwill has tried to read the Bible and ended up putting it down in utter confusion. It helps to have a companion, and *Liguori Catholic Bible Study* is a solid one. Over the course of this series, you'll learn about biblical messages, themes, personalities, and events and understand how the books of the Bible rose out of the need to address new situations.

Across the centuries, people of faith have asked, "Where is God in this moment?" Millions of Catholics look to the Bible for encouragement in their journey of faith. Wisdom teaches us not to undertake Bible study alone, disconnected from the Church that was given Scripture to share and treasure. When used as a source of prayer and thoughtful reflection, the Bible comes alive.

Your choice of a Bible-study program should be dictated by what you want to get out of it. One goal of *Liguori Catholic Bible Study* is to give readers greater familiarity with the Bible's structure, themes, personalities, and message. But that's not enough. This program will also teach you to use Scripture in your prayer. God's message is as compelling and urgent today as ever, but we get only part of the message when it's memorized and stuck in our heads. It's meant for the entire person—physical, emotional, and spiritual.

We're baptized into life with Christ, and we're called to live more fully with Christ today as we practice the values of justice, peace, forgiveness, and community. God's new covenant was written on the hearts of the people of Israel; we, their spiritual descendants, are loved that intimately by God today. *Liguori Catholic Bible Study* will draw you closer to God, in whose image and likeness we are fashioned.

Group and Individual Study

The *Liguori Catholic Bible Study* series is intended for group and individual study and prayer. This series gives you the tools to start a study group. Gathering two or three people in a home or announcing the meeting of a Bible-study group in a parish or community can bring surprising results. Each lesson in this series contains a section to help groups study, reflect, pray, and share biblical reflections. Each lesson but the first also has a second section for individual study.

Many people who want to learn more about the Bible don't know where to begin. This series gives them a place to start and helps them continue until they're familiar with all the books of the Bible.

Bible study can be a lifelong project, always enriching those who wish to be faithful to God's Word. When people complete a study of the whole Bible, they can begin again, making new discoveries with each new adventure into the Word of God.

Lectio Divina
(Sacred Reading)

BIBLE STUDY isn't just a matter of gaining intellectual knowledge of the Bible; it's also about gaining a greater understanding of God's love and concern for creation. The purpose of reading and knowing the Bible is to enrich our relationship with God. God loves us and gave us the Bible to illustrate that love. In his April 12, 2013, address before the Pontifical Biblical Commission, Pope Francis stressed that "the Church's life and mission are founded on the word of God which is the soul of theology and at the same time inspires the whole of Christian life."

The Meaning of *Lectio Divina*

Lectio divina is a Latin expression that means "divine or sacred reading." The process for *lectio divina* consists of Scripture readings, reflection, and prayer. Many clergy, religious, and laity use *lectio divina* in their daily spiritual reading to develop a closer and more loving relationship with God. Learning about Scripture has as its purpose the living of its message, which demands a period of reflection on Scripture passages.

Prayer and *Lectio Divina*

Prayer is a necessary element for the practice of *lectio divina*. The entire process of reading and reflecting is a prayer. It's not merely an intellectual pursuit; it's also a spiritual one. Page 16 includes an opening prayer for gathering one's thoughts before moving on to the passages in each section. This prayer may be used privately or in a group. For those who use the book for daily spiritual reading, the prayer for each section may be repeated each day. Some may wish to keep a journal of each day's meditation.

Pondering the Word of God

Lectio divina is the ancient Christian spiritual practice of reading the holy Scriptures with intentionality and devotion. This practice helps Christians center themselves and descend to the level of the heart to enter an inner quiet space, finding God.

This sacred reading is distinct from reading for knowledge or information, and it's more than the pious practice of spiritual reading. It is the practice of opening ourselves to the action and inspiration of the Holy Spirit. As we intentionally focus on and become present to the inner meaning of the Scripture passage, the Holy Spirit enlightens our minds and hearts. We come to the text willing to be influenced by a deeper meaning that lies within the words and thoughts we ponder.

In this space, we open ourselves to be challenged and changed by the inner meaning we experience. We approach the text in a spirit of faith and obedience as a disciple ready to be taught by the Holy Spirit. As we savor the sacred text, we let go of our usual control of how we expect God to act in our lives and surrender our heart and conscience to the flow of the divine (*divina*) through the reading (*lectio*).

The fundamental principle of *lectio divina* leads us to understand the profound mystery of the Incarnation, "The Word became flesh," not only in history but also within us.

Praying *Lectio* Today

Before you begin, relax your body and maintain a posture of prayer (back straight, eyes shut, feet flat on the floor). Then practice these four simple actions:

1. Read a passage from Scripture or the daily Mass readings. This is known as *lectio*. (If the Word of God is read aloud, the hearers listen attentively.)

2. Pray the selected passage with attention as you listen for a specific meaning that comes to mind. Once again, the reading is listened to or silently read and reflected or meditated on. This is known as *meditatio*.

3. The exercise becomes active. Pick a word, sentence, or idea that surfaces from your consideration of the chosen text. Does the reading remind you of a person, place, or experience? If so, pray about it. Compose your thoughts and reflection into a simple word or phrase. This prayer-thought will help you remove distractions during the *lectio*. This exercise is called *oratio*.

4. In silence, with your eyes closed, quiet yourself and become conscious of your breathing. Let your thoughts, feelings, and concerns fade as you consider the selected passage in the previous step (*oratio*). If you're distracted, use your prayer word to help you return to silence. This is *contemplatio*.

This exercise can take as long as you want, but in the context of this Bible study, 10 to 20 minutes should be sufficient.

Many teachers of prayer call contemplation the prayer of resting in God, a prelude to losing oneself in the presence of God. Scripture is transformed in our hearing as we pray and allow our hearts to unite intimately with the Lord. The Word truly takes on flesh, and this time it is manifested in our flesh.

How to Use This Bible-Study Companion

THE BIBLE, along with the commentaries and reflections found in this study, will help participants become familiar with the Scripture texts and lead them to reflect more deeply on the texts' messages. At the end of this study, participants will have a firm grasp of the Universal Letters and realize how these letters offer spiritual nourishment. This study is not only an intellectual adventure, it's also a spiritual one. The reflections lead participants into their own journey with the Scripture readings.

Context

When the authors wrote and edited the Universal Letters, they were dealing with later developments within Christianity that earlier writers of the New Testament did not experience, perceive, or address. To help readers learn about each passage in relation to those around it, each lesson begins with an overview that puts the Scripture passages into context.

Part 1: Group Study

To give participants a comprehensive study of the Universal Letters, the book is divided into six lessons. Lesson 1 is group study only; Lessons 2 through 6 are divided into Part 1, group study, and Part 2, individual study. For example, Lesson 2 covers James 2:14—5. The study group reads and discusses only James 2:14—4:12 (Part 1). Participants privately read and reflect on chapter 4:13–17 and all of chapter 5 (Part 2).

Group study may or may not include *lectio divina*. With *lectio divina*, the group meets for ninety minutes using the first format on page 14. Without *lectio divina*, the group meets for one hour using the format at the bottom of page 14, and participants are urged to privately read the *lectio divina* section at the end of Part 1. It contains additional reflections on the Scripture passages studied during the group session that will take participants even further into the passages.

Part 2: Individual Study

The passages not covered in Part 1 are divided into shorter components, one to be studied each day. Participants who don't belong to a study group can use the lessons for private sacred reading. They may choose to reflect on one Scripture passage per day, making it possible for a clearer understanding of the Scripture passages used in their *lectio divina* (sacred reading).

A PROCESS FOR SACRED READING

Liguori Publications has designed this study to be user-friendly and manageable. However, group dynamics and leaders vary. We're not trying to keep the Holy Spirit from working in your midst, thus we suggest you decide beforehand which format works best for your group. If you have limited time, you could study the Bible as a group and save prayer and reflection for personal time.

However, if your group wishes to digest and feast on sacred Scripture through both prayer and study, we recommend you spend closer to ninety minutes each week by gathering to study and pray with Scripture. *Lectio divina* (see page 9) is an ancient contemplative prayer form that moves readers from the head to the heart in meeting the Lord. We strongly suggest using this prayer form whether in individual or group study.

GROUP-STUDY FORMATS

1. Bible Study With *Lectio Divina*
About ninety minutes of group study
- ✠ Gathering and opening prayer (3–5 minutes)
- ✠ Read Scripture passage aloud (5 minutes)
- ✠ Silently review the commentary and prepare to discuss it with the group (3–5 minutes)
- ✠ Discuss the Scripture passage along with the commentary and reflection (30 minutes)
- ✠ Read each Scripture passage aloud a second time, followed by quiet time for meditation and contemplation (5 minutes)
- ✠ Spend some time in prayer with the selected passage. Group participants will slowly read the Scripture passage a third time in silence, listening for the voice of God as they read (10–20 minutes)
- ✠ Shared reflection (10–15 minutes)
- ✠ Closing prayer (3–5 minutes)

To become acquainted with lectio divina, *see page 9.*

2. Bible Study
About one hour of group study
- ✠ Gathering and opening prayer (3–5 minutes)
- ✠ Read each Scripture passage aloud (5 minutes)
- ✠ Silently review the commentary and prepare to discuss it with the group (3–5 minutes)
- ✠ Discuss the Scripture passage along with the commentary and reflection (40 minutes)
- ✠ Closing prayer (3–5 minutes)

Notes to the Leader

- ✠ Bring a copy of the *New American Bible,* revised edition.
- ✠ Plan which sections will be covered each week of your Bible study.
- ✠ Read the material in advance of each lesson.
- ✠ Establish written ground rules. (Example: We won't keep you longer than ninety minutes; don't dominate the sharing by arguing or debating.)
- ✠ Meet in an appropriate and welcoming gathering space (church building, meeting room, house).
- ✠ Provide name tags and perhaps use a brief icebreaker for the first meeting; ask participants to introduce themselves.
- ✠ Mark the Scripture passage(s) that will be read during the session.
- ✠ Decide how you would like the Scripture to be read aloud (whether by one or multiple readers).
- ✠ Use a clock or watch.
- ✠ Provide extra Bibles (or copies of the Scripture passages) for participants who don't bring their Bible.
- ✠ Ask participants to read "Introduction: The Universal Letters" (page 17) before the first session.
- ✠ Tell participants which passages to study and urge them to read the passages and commentaries before the meeting.
- ✠ If you opt to use the *lectio divina* format, familiarize yourself with this prayer form ahead of time.

Notes to Participants

- ✠ Bring a copy of the *New American Bible,* revised edition.
- ✠ Read "Introduction: The Universal Letters" (page 17) before the first lesson.
- ✠ Read the Scripture passages and commentaries before each lesson.
- ✠ Be prepared to share and listen respectfully. (This is not a time to debate beliefs or argue.)

Opening Prayer

Leader: O God, come to my assistance.

Response: O Lord, make haste to help me.

Leader: Glory be to the Father, and to the Son, and to the Holy Spirit…

Response: …as it was in the beginning, is now, and ever shall be, world without end. Amen.

Leader: Christ is the vine and we are the branches. As branches linked to Jesus, the vine, we are called to recognize that the Scriptures are always being fulfilled in our lives. It is the living Word of God living on in us. Come, Holy Spirit, fill the hearts of your faithful and kindle in us the fire of your divine wisdom, knowledge, and love.

Response: Open our minds and hearts as we study your great love for us as shown in the Bible.

Reader: (Open your Bible to the assigned Scripture(s) and read in a paced, deliberate manner. Pause for one minute, listening for a word, phrase, or image that you may use in your *lectio divina* practice.)

Closing Prayer

Leader: Let us pray as Jesus taught us.

Response: Our Father…

Leader: Lord, inspire us with your Spirit as we study your Word in the Bible. Be with us this day and every day as we strive to know you and serve you and to love as you love. We believe that through your goodness and love, the Spirit of the Lord is truly upon us. Allow the words of the Bible, your Word, to capture us and inspire us to live as you live and to love as you love.

Response: Amen.

Leader: May the divine assistance remain with us always.

Response: In the name of the Father, and of the Son, and of the Holy Spirit. Amen.

The Universal Letters

Read this overview before the first session.

A COUPLE CELEBRATING their fortieth wedding anniversary decided to travel from New York to California, stopping at major hotels on their journey. In several of the hotels, they would turn on their television and find a note on the screen telling them they had a message. When they tuned in to the message, they would read a note that began, "Dear Guests," which would then welcome them to the hotel and wish them an enjoyable rest during their visit. The couple, knowing the message was a general one received by all the newly arrived guests at the hotel, knew the manager of the hotel did not write that letter specifically for them. It was a common form letter welcoming those who chose to stay at that hotel.

In the early Church, several New Testament authors wrote general letters to those who shared faith in Jesus Christ, instructing or encouraging them in their faith. For instance, when the author of the Gospel of Luke began his Gospel, he addressed it to someone named "Theophilus." Many commentators believe the name Theophilus was a fictitious name used to designate all those who loved God. The name means "friend of God" or "lover of God." This was the author's way of saying that his Gospel was a universal Gospel, meant not only for Jewish converts to Christianity but for all believers, Jews as well as Gentiles. The genealogy in Luke's Gospel does not trace back to Abraham, the father of the Israelite nation, as found in Matthew's Gospel, but it goes back beyond Abraham to Adam and Eve, the biblical first parents of all human creation. It was a Gospel for all believers on their journey in the faith.

The Catholic or Universal Letters

Among the New Testament letters, some are addressed to general audiences, just as the Gospel of Luke was addressed to a general audience under the name of Theophilus. Because the authors of the letters in this volume were addressing a general audience, the letters became known as the Catholic or Universal Letters. In its earliest meaning, the word "catholic" did not refer to a specific denomination among Christian churches, but it was another word for "universal." The Catholic or Universal Letters embrace seven letters of the New Testament that include a letter attributed to James (mentioned in the New Testament as a brother of Jesus—see Mark 6:3), two letters attributed to Peter, three attributed to John, and one attributed to Jude.

The author of James addresses his letter to the twelve tribes of the dispersion, an apparent reference to Christians spread throughout the known world. The author of 1 Peter addresses his letter to a number of churches in Asia Minor, while the author of 2 Peter addresses his letter to "those who have received a faith of equal value to ours through the righteousness of our God and savior Jesus Christ" (2 Peter 1:1).

In 1 John, the author does not address his letter to anyone, but he does speak of his readers as "my children" (1 John 2:1). The Second Letter of John is addressed to a "chosen Lady and to her children," a reference that many commentators believe refers to the Church in general (see 2 John 1:1). Although the author of 3 John addresses his letter to an unknown specific individual named Gaius, the name Gaius was sometimes used in letters for addressing a general group of Christians, just as the author of the Gospel of Luke used the name Theophilus to address his letter to a universal audience. The author of Jude addresses his letter "to those who are called, beloved in God the Father and kept safe for Jesus Christ" (Jude 1:1).

For a period of time, the early Church hesitated to include these letters in the New Testament due to a widespread question concerning the authenticity of the authors. The hesitation rested on the belief that the apostolic tradition of the Scriptures depended on the authenticity of the author as an immediate follower of Jesus, someone who traveled with him or knew him during his sojourn on earth. In time, the Church realized that the acceptance of a work as coming from the apostolic tradition did not depend on the name of the author as much as it did on the depository of the faith. The leaders of the early Church determined that the works remained faithful to the teachings of the authors whose name they bore. By the end of the fourth and early fifth centuries, the Greek and Latin Churches accepted the letters as part of the revealed Scriptures.

The Johannine Community

Although many commentators believe that the Universal Letters were not written by the authors to whom they were attributed, the people named had a real influence on the development of the letters. For instance, the letters of Peter appear to reflect the thinking of Peter and may have come from followers who belonged to a community faithful to the teachings of Peter the Apostle. The author is addressing situations that did not exist when Peter lived and the basic concepts still remained faithful to Peter's original teachings. The same may be true of the Letter of James. The three letters of John apparently come from a community known to scholars as the Johannine community. This community remained faithful to the teachings of John the Apostle.

In recent years, an extensive amount of study has been done concerning the Johannine school of the New Testament. The term "school" used in this context does not mean that the writers all went to class to learn what John taught, but it refers to a school of thought, a manner of thinking that remained faithful to the original teachings of John and developed according to particular historical and community situations addressed by the author. This school is represented in the three letters of John as well as in the Gospel of John. Although these letters may have been written by different authors, they share many similar theological concepts.

Understanding the development of the Johannine school enables us to understand the similarities and differences found in the Gospel of John and the Letters of John. Small communities arose within Christianity shortly after the resurrection of Jesus, and it is likely that most were originally under the leadership of those followers of Jesus who were eye-witnesses to Christ's ministry. An understanding of the development of the Johannine school, which was most extensively studied and identified, can offer insights into the development of the letters allegedly written by James and Peter.

The Johannine community developed over several stages, and its history is complex. It began as a Jewish community comprising early followers of Jesus in or around Palestine. Some of John the Baptist's followers also joined this community. Many later converts became part of the Johannine community, including Gentiles from areas outside Palestine who were greatly influenced by the Greek culture.

In the midst of a persecution that took place after the destruction of Jerusalem in 70 AD and the expulsion of Christians from the synagogues, evangelists collected the traditions of the Jewish Christian community and interpreted them for the Christian community that was now obviously separated from Judaism.

Other later followers of Jesus' teachings became part of the Johannine community. The Johannine community was not confined to one geographical area as though it was a community of monks living together. Evangelists carried the original Johannine message from one community to another, and these communities applied the basic message to their own historical circumstances.

The final form of John's Gospel and the letters found in the New Testament, which were allegedly written by John, came as a result of many of the ideas and writings of the early Johannine community produced by editors. The characteristics of the theology of the Johannine letters have much in common with those found in the introduction to John's

Gospel, although they are most likely not written by the same author. Just as the developments found in the Johannine community help us understand how the Gospel and the letters can be attributed to John, so a close study of the Universal Letters by Scripture scholars revealed how they followed the basic ideas and teachings of the person whose name they bear.

Be Doers of the Word

JAMES 1—2:13

So speak and so act as people who will be judged by the law of freedom. For the judgment is merciless to one who has not shown mercy; mercy triumphs over judgment (2:12–13).

Opening Prayer (SEE PAGE 16)

Context

Although the Letter of James begins with a greeting, it is not properly a letter. Since it lacks any kind of proclamation, we cannot even call it a sermon. Instead, the author follows the custom of offering moral directives for his audience, and his letter contains very little that could be specifically considered Christian. Even when the author mentions the name of Jesus Christ, which he does twice, those citations could be omitted without any effect on the direction of the thought presented. The letter concerns itself with living a holy life within the community and presents a series of proverbs and exhortations directed toward living such a life.

Although the Letter of James seems to come from a Jewish author, the author writes in a highly skilled Greek style. If James, the head of the Church at Jerusalem, is the author, then he must have depended on a secretary to write the letter as he dictated it, which was a custom occasionally used in the early centuries. More recent commentators doubt that James is the author of the letter, since the author does not mention anything about the background of James, nor does he place any emphasis on Mosaic Law.

The author speaks of himself as a slave of God and of the Lord Jesus Christ. He encourages his readers to persevere in the midst of trials for the sake of becoming perfect and urges them to pray for wisdom with a trusting faith. The poor should recognize their high standing, and the rich should recognize their lowliness. Perseverance in the midst of temptation leads to holiness. God is never the source of one's temptation, but the source is one's own desires. A constant theme of the letter is one should be a doer of the Word (God's Word) and not only a hearer.

The author urges readers to control their tongues (not gossiping or slandering), and to support orphans and widows. They are to show no partiality, recognizing that the Lord chose those who are poor in the world to be rich in faith and heirs of God's kingdom, and they are to show mercy, since mercy triumphs over judgment.

GROUP STUDY (JAMES 1—2:13)

Read aloud James 1—2:13.

1:1 A Slave of God

In the opening line of the letter, the author identifies himself as a man named James. At the beginning of the letter, James does not identify himself as an apostle of the Lord, therefore the letter appears to be attributed to a later James who was not one of the Twelve. Some identify the author as the one referred to in Paul's Letter to the Galatians as "James the brother of the Lord" (Galatians 1:19). If James, the brother of the Lord, were the author of the letter, he would then be the leader of the Jewish Christian community in Jerusalem and would be the designated leader of the early Christians, the one to whom Paul would report in seeking to free the Gentiles from the Mosaic Law. The term "brother" in Jesus' era could refer to any male who was a relative of Jesus, such as a cousin.

Many commentators believe the letter, although supposedly written by someone named James, was written by an anonymous author who chose the name James to give the letter authority. The letter, which contains material that does not demand an eyewitness, was written by an author with a good knowledge of the Greek language. Since James, "the brother of Jesus," was a Jew who lived in Jerusalem, he would most likely have been more comfortable with the Hebrew language than with Greek and would have written in that language. The author of James is unknown.

The author, after identifying himself, speaks of himself as being a slave of God and of the Lord Jesus Christ. All the disciples of the New Testament era saw themselves as slaves or servants of the Lord. This title is both a sign of servitude and honor. The members of the early Church considered it an honor to be called to serve the Lord. Paul the Apostle often began his letters in the same manner, identifying himself as a "slave of Christ Jesus" (Romans 1:1). Paul and the author of James dedicated their lives totally to the Lord as slaves dedicated their lives to their masters.

The author addresses his letter to "the twelve tribes in the dispersion" (1:1). The reference to the dispersion or Diaspora has its roots in Israelite history. In 587 BC, the Babylonians invaded Jerusalem, forcing many inhabitants to flee to other countries. Many who did not flee were led into exile in Babylon. Seventy years later, Cyrus the Persian conquered the Babylonians and allowed the Israelites to return home, but not all returned. Many of those born and raised in Babylon chose to remain in the only land they knew.

Most of those who fled to other countries to avoid the Babylonian invasion also chose to remain in the colonies they established outside their homeland. The Babylonian conquests and other tragedies of history that forced the people to flee from Judea led to the establishment of Jewish communities outside Palestine that existed to and beyond the time of Christ. The movement involving all those who fled also became part of "the dispersion."

The reference to the twelve tribes of Israel has its roots in the twelve tribes making up the Israelite nation at the time the nation settled in the Promised Land. These were descendants from the twelve sons of Jacob. Many people living outside Palestine no longer spoke their native Hebrew language and learned the language and customs of the Greek culture in which they lived without abandoning their Jewish beliefs. The dispersion provided an opportunity for the evangelists of the early Church to spread the faith among the Jews of the dispersion and convert many of them to Christ. They already knew the Old Testament and lived with the expectation of a Messiah.

The Jews living in Jerusalem during Jesus' era were aware of these communities, which were established outside Palestine. In John's Gospel, when Jesus announced to the Jews of Judah that he would be leaving for a place where they could not come, they responded, "Surely he is not going to the dispersion among the Greeks to teach the Greeks" (John 7:35). The author of the Gospel of John could be cleverly using the occasion of Jesus' departure from the world to infer that Jesus' message would spread among the Jews of the dispersion and their Greek neighbors. Jesus himself did not leave to go to the Greek-speaking Jews, but his disciples carried his message outside of Israel to the Greek-speaking world.

Some commentators believe the letter had a larger focus, one beyond this world that was addressed to Christians who were exiles from their true home, heaven. The early followers of Christ identified themselves as the new Israel. In this case, "the twelve tribes of the dispersion" found in James would refer to all Christians, the new Israel, those living outside Israel.

1:2–11 Perseverance in Temptation

In this section, and throughout the letter, the author uses catchwords to move from one theme to another. He first speaks of trials and temptation, then to endurance in persecution, and subsequently to perfect perseverance. He reminds his readers that although they will endure trials, these trials should be seen as joyful opportunities for testing one's faith. The trials here refer to the daily difficulties Christians had to endure rather than any particular persecution. The faith that will later be proved is not allegiance to a specific belief as much as it is the living of one's faith. The faithful endurance of these trials will lead to patience.

Perseverance, then, becomes the next message's catchword. Just as trials offer opportunities to prove oneself, so perseverance also offers an opportunity for one to come to perfection. The perfection spoken of in this section refers to constancy or endurance rather than to a lack of any fault. This perfection will lead to spiritual maturity and leave a person lacking nothing.

Wisdom is the catchword for the next idea. For those who lack wisdom, the author offers words of encouragement, urging readers to ask for this gift from God, who gives generously and ungrudgingly to all. The wisdom mentioned here does not refer to worldly wisdom as much as it does to the wisdom of knowing God and serving in God's creation. The reader must ask for wisdom in faith, without any hesitation or doubt. Jesus said, "Therefore I tell you, all that you ask for in prayer, believe that you will receive it and it shall be yours" (Mark 11:24). God is willing to provide true wisdom to believers who seek it.

The author likens the doubting person to the waves of the sea driven by the wind. Because such people are double-minded and unstable like the sea, they cannot expect anything from the Lord. They seek wisdom but lack the ability to trust that God will provide it.

The author makes use of contrasts in his letter by speaking of the difference between the poor and the rich. The poor can boast of their lowly condition because of their high position before God, while the rich, because their wealth lasts no longer than a flower in the field, have no reason to boast. The author describes how the sun rises, the grass and flowers wither, and the beauty of the meadow disappears. This imagery has the overtones of judgment attached to it.

The rich, who are divided among many projects of the world, will wither away in the midst of all their pursuits. Isaiah the prophet reminds us that we live in a passing world: "All flesh is grass, and all their loyalty like the flower of the field. The grass withers, the flower wilts, when the breath of the LORD blows upon it" (Isaiah 40:6–7). Only the Word of the Lord endures.

1:12–18 The Crown of Life

The author returns to the concept of trials (temptations) that he mentions at the opening of this letter. The person who remains faithful through temptation will receive the crown of life promised to those who love the Lord. The crown of life refers to the victor's crown that was awarded in ancient times to the one deserving of such honor. This message recalls the Beatitudes found in the Gospel of Matthew (see 5:1–11). Those who remain faithful will receive the crown of life promised to those who love the Lord.

Although the author sees temptation as leading to joyful results in the Lord, he insists that temptation cannot be said to come from God. God, who is not able to be tempted, would certainly not tempt others. The source of all temptations comes from within a person, from the allurements and seductions of one's own desires. These desires, once conceived, give birth to sin, and sin—once fully matured—brings death.

Lest one believe that the Lord is the source of temptations and death, the author tells us that the Lord bestows every good and perfect gift that comes from above. The contrast between temptation and goodness is meant to be a contrast between one's inner pull toward sinfulness and death and God's goodness. The gift from God comes from the one called the "Father of lights," that is, the Creator of the lights of the heavens. Unlike these heavenly lights, God cannot change and be overshadowed. By God's own choice, we are brought to birth by God's creative Word of truth. In this way, we become, as Christians, the first fruits of God's new creation in the risen Christ.

1:19–27 Be Doers of the Word

The author shares some practical ways of living the faith, telling his readers to pay attention to what he is about to say. He tells his hearers to be quick to listen, slow to speak, slow to anger, which means that a person should listen with openness to God's Word, act well according to it, and not allow one's anger to explode. Anger does not produce God's righteousness. In using the term "righteousness" here, the author is referring to the good works that God asks of us. Anger blocks the performance of these good deeds.

The author then exhorts his readers to do away with all filth, evil, and wickedness. In contrast to stripping away all evil, Christians must welcome the seed of the Gospel that was implanted in them and has the power to save them. This acceptance of the Word does not consist in simply hearing it, but putting it into action. To clarify his point, the author uses an image of a person looking in a mirror. A person who simply hears the Word and does not put it into action is like a person who looks into a mirror and, turning away, forgets what he or she looks like. Jesus said, "And everyone who listens to these words of mine but does not act on them will be like a fool who built his house on sand" (Matthew 7:26). To listen to the Word and not act on it is to forget the meaning of the Word in one's life. In contrast, those who understand the perfect law of freedom and persevere are not hearers who forget but doers who act. Those who do this will be blessed. The author contrasts looking into the mirror and seeing oneself with peering into the mirror and seeing the perfect law of God.

The author then states that the living of the Word involves being slow to speak, meaning that those who speak should control their tongue, not allowing their words to hurt another. Those who cannot control their speech should not consider themselves religious. True faith and worship of God consist in living the faith. The author names some of those concerns that were considered important in both Old and New Testament times. The first of these concerns is for widows and orphans. Besides caring for these people who are in need, the author also urges his readers to keep themselves unstained by the world, which is a sign of true worship of God. When he speaks of being unstained by the world, he is using the image of the world in the sense of worldly concerns overwhelming concerns directed toward salvation.

2:1–13 Showing Partiality

The author now speaks out against partiality among Christians. Christians have faith in the Lord Jesus Christ, and they know that Jesus showed no partiality. In the Gospel of Matthew, we read that Jesus proved to John the Baptist his call to be the one who is to come by showing no partiality. He told John's disciples to go and report to John that "the blind regain their sight, the lame walk, lepers are cleansed, the deaf hear, the dead are raised, and the poor have the good news proclaimed to them" (Matthew 11:5). All receive the gifts of Christ equally.

The author of James tells his readers that some may act differently toward the rich and the poor. He contrasts an image of a rich man with rings on his fingers and fine clothing coming into an assembly and a poor man in shabby clothes coming into the same assembly. He portrays the rich man as being invited to take a seat, while the poor man is being left standing or invited to sit at the host's feet. He questions his readers, asking if they are able to see how they have discriminated against the poor and set themselves up as corrupt judges.

The author calls his readers to listen to his words, questioning whether they recognize that God chose those who are poor (according to the world's norms) to be the ones rich in faith and heirs of the kingdom that was promised to those who love God. He recalls that his readers treated the poor without dignity. The rich dragged them into court and blasphemed the name by which they themselves were baptized.

The answer the author offers to his readers is not that they should reject the rich in favor of the poor but that they should fulfill the law of love, which the author refers to as a royal law. He may be using this image of a royal law since it comes from God. They should love their neighbor, rich or poor, as themselves. Any sign of partiality or favoritism marks them as sinners, condemned by the law itself.

The word "law" leads to a development of another idea concerning the breaking of the law, namely that the person who breaks one aspect of the law breaks the whole law. The same Lord who told them not to commit adultery also told them not to kill. The person who does not commit adultery but who kills is guilty of breaking the law.

Christians should speak and act in expectation of being judged by the law of liberty, which is a law of love. Only by fulfilling the command of love can the whole law be fulfilled. Just as Jesus was able to say in the Gospel of Matthew that the merciful are blessed and will receive mercy (see Matthew 5:7), so the author of James is able to state that those who have not shown mercy will receive a merciless judgment. The merciful need not fear judgment, since "mercy triumphs over judgment." (James 2:13)

Review Questions

1. What does the author mean when he says he is a slave of God and the Lord Jesus Christ?
2. Why should Christians rejoice when they encounter various trials in their life?
3. How does the author of the letter expect people of lowly circumstances to take pride in their high standing?
4. Does God tempt us?
5. How can we be doers of the Word and not merely hearers?
6. Name examples of partiality that people exhibit in our culture.

Closing Prayer (SEE PAGE 16)

Pray the closing prayer now or after *lectio divina.*

Lectio Divina (SEE PAGE 9)

Relax your body and maintain a posture of prayer (back straight, eyes shut, feet flat on the floor). This exercise can take as long as you want, but in the context of this Bible study, 10 to 20 minutes should be sufficient.

The meditations that follow are provided only to help group participants use this prayer form, but note that *lectio* is intended to bring one to a place of prayerful contemplation where the Word of God speaks to the hearer from his or her heart. (See page 9 for further instruction.)

A Slave of God (1:1)

Saint Damien of Molokai (1840–1849) offered himself as a slave of God and the Lord Jesus Christ when he volunteered to minister to people afflicted with leprosy in a leper colony on the Island of Molokai in Hawaii, knowing that he risked being exiled from his homeland because of his contact with the afflicted exiles on the island. At that time in history, there was no cure for leprosy, and people had no idea how the dreaded disease was spread.

During Damien's time on the island, he performed a number of ministries besides preaching the Gospel. He helped the people build, repair, and paint homes and dressed the wounds of the afflicted. One day, while stepping into hot water, he felt nothing and realized that he himself had become a victim of leprosy, a wounded healer. He was now one with the people on the island. Despite his leprosy, he continued to help others in the colony until his death at age forty-nine.

Many people in the world soon learned of the dedication of Father Damien. Following Father Damien's example, others volunteered to minister to those in need of comfort and healing, even in the face of difficult and dangerous situations. Father Damien had a mission, but another mission grew out of his ministry, namely the ministry of example, leading others to live as slaves for Jesus Christ.

The author of James opens his letter by stating that he is a "slave of God and of the Lord Jesus Christ," and he writes to a general audience dispersed throughout the world of his time. Father Damien offered himself as a slave of Jesus Christ, and his example lives on like a letter to people throughout our world today who willingly volunteer to follow his model of love and dedication to the people for the sake of Jesus Christ.

✠ *What can I learn from this passage?*

Perseverance in Temptation (1:2–11)

In the Gospel of Luke, we read that the devil tempted Jesus by taking him to a very high mountain and showing him all the kingdoms of the world. He promised to give Jesus the world and all its magnificence if Jesus would fall down and worship him. Jesus overcame the temptation by telling Satan a person shall worship and serve God alone (see Luke 4:5–8). When we see how far Christianity has spread throughout the world, we recognize that Jesus has indeed gained the world by rejecting Satan's temptation. He did not gain personal wealth or power, but he gained salvation for all people who are willing to accept it.

Saint Francis of Assisi offers another example of gaining the whole world while losing material wealth. He belonged to a wealthy family and had all the luxuries one could want in life. He could have enjoyed the magnificence of his wealth, but he chose to reject it all and trust in the Lord by becoming a poor beggar and founder of the Franciscan Order. If Francis decided to live the life of luxury his wealth could bring, we might never know about him today. He would be just another rich man who passed away into the unknown files of history, as happened to many rich people before and after him. By choosing poverty, he founded a religious order that brought the faith to many people of the world and changed history by converting countless numbers of people to Christ. We could say that he gained the spiritual magnificence of the world, as Jesus did, by dedicating his life to the Lord rather than to his riches.

The author of James stresses the wisdom of perseverance in serving the Lord, knowing that the rich will pass away like a flower in a field, while those who dedicate themselves to the Lord will make a major difference in God's creation.

✠ *What can I learn from this passage?*

The Crown of Life (1:12–18)

In the Lord's Prayer, we pray, "lead us not into temptation." Some mistakenly think the phrase means the Lord would lead us into temptation if we did not pray. No. It means the Lord will not allow us to be tested beyond our strength.

Examples of such testing took place during the Vietnam War. A Christian-Vietnamese father would tell his family members to pray each night that they would not be tested by some tragedy. During the war, some Vietnamese rebels would invade a village, carry off the young women, and kill others. Families feared that they would awaken and find that some family members had been taken away. Many feared this test would be too severe for them, and they prayed that they would not have to endure such a test. For them, "lead us not into temptation" was a prayer that the Lord would protect them from such a horrible family tragedy.

As the author of James tells us, God does not tempt us or cause such a test, but if it should happen, what would happen to our faith in God? It would be the ultimate test. When we pray that we will not be led into temptation, we are actually praying for strength in times of temptation and testing. Good things come from the Lord, not evil. Evil comes from evil. Although we have difficulties in life, we should never neglect to thank the Lord for all the good gifts we have received.

✠ *What can I learn from this passage?*

Be Doers of the Word (1:19–27)

A religious organization decided to purchase some advertising time on television to convey a message about helping others. One of their advertisements showed the picture of an elderly woman in her apartment moving curtains aside and peering out the window. She obviously lived alone. From the distant street below could be heard horns and sirens, signs that she lived in the midst of a bustling city. Then there was a knock at the door. She turned, smiled a bit, and showed that she was hoping for some company. As she turned toward the door, an unseen voice asked, "Is it ever you?" The advertisement ends there!

We hear a great deal about helping others, but we can become too busy to write a card, make a phone call, visit an elderly relative or neighbor, or help people with their groceries. The world is filled with lonely people who ask nothing more than someone to pay attention to them in some manner. We can worship weekly, but we all have to answer the question when it comes to putting our faith into action, "Is it ever you?" As the author of James tells us, we have the call to be doers of the Word, not just hearers.

✠ *What can I learn from this passage?*

Showing Partiality (2:1–13)

A story about a highly successful African American baseball player appeared in a national magazine. It said the player went into a furniture store to purchase a living-room set for his elderly parents. He wanted to surprise them with an expensive set of furniture for their home. Before he came to the store, he finished a workout and was dressed in jeans and tennis shoes.

A salesperson, who knew nothing about baseball, judged that the man was looking for inexpensive furniture, and he took him immediately to the thrift section of the store. A moment later, another man, well-dressed and obviously well-to-do, came into the store and was shown to a more expensive display on the other side of the showroom. The salesperson spent a considerable amount of time with the well-dressed man and ignored the baseball player.

The player, becoming angry with the attitude of the salesperson, went over to him, opened his wallet to show that he intended to pay the total expense of the furniture in cash, and then he left the store. The wealthy man saw what happened and decided that he also would not deal with a salesperson who showed such disregard for someone who looked poor.

The event shows the attitude many people have toward the rich and the poor. The author of James reminds people that the Lord is present in all people. He warns them against the sin of partiality. To dishonor the poor is to dishonor the Lord, and to break one of the Lord's commands concerning love of neighbor is equivalent to breaking all the commandments. The bottom line is that we should treat all people equally, never judging, and realizing that mercy toward all—no matter what their status in society may be—allows the Lord to treat us with mercy. As the author of James tells us, mercy overcomes judgment.

✠ *What can I learn from this passage?*

Faith Without Works Is Dead

JAMES 2:14—5

If a brother or sister has nothing to wear and has no food for the day, and one of you says to them, "Go in peace, keep warm, and eat well," but you do not give them the necessities of the body, what good is it? So also faith of itself, if it does not have works, is dead (2:15–17).

Opening Prayer (SEE PAGE 16)

Context

Part 1: James 2:14—4:12 The author of the Letter of James tells us that faith without works is dead. If people have particular needs and another person does nothing for them except wish them well, what good is that? A person's works show whether or not that person is acting with or without faith. Abraham's willingness to sacrifice his son Isaac is an example of a work that showed Abraham's faith. Faith and works exist as one. Abraham demonstrates how both works and faith, not faith alone, are necessary. Rahab, who saved the spies sent into the Promised Land by Joshua, showed by her works that she had faith.

Just as a horse needs someone to control the whole horse by the use of a bridle, and a ship with a rudder needs someone to steer the whole ship, so the tongue—as small as it is—controls the whole person. Like a fire, the tongue can set the course of one's life on fire and lead to the fires of Gehenna. We can bless the Lord with our tongue and with the same tongue curse other humans. We should practice wisdom that is from above and avoid all sinful inclinations. Causes of divisions come from love of the world above love of God. Since there is one lawgiver and judge who is the Lord, who are we to judge our neighbor? The present time, not some future time, is the time to change one's life and live close to the Lord.

Part 2: James 4:13—5 It is time for the rich to lament, since they have lived a life of luxury and pleasure and have fattened them-selves for the Day of Judgment. Like the farmer who must wait for the harvest, the followers of the Lord must be patient and firm in their commitment to the Lord. They are to avoid complaining and must persevere as did prophets like Job. They are to make their "yes" mean "yes," and their "no" mean "no," being honest enough so they have no need of swearing to the truth.

Those who are sick should summon the presbyters of the Church to pray and anoint them with oil in the name of the Lord. Their prayer of faith will raise the sick person up and forgive sins. Confession of one's sins and perseverance and trust in prayer are very power-ful for the just person. Elijah's prayer for the cessation of rain was answered because he believed (see 1 Kings 17:1). The one who brings back a sinner will save his or her soul, and such action will cover a multitude of sins.

PART 1: GROUP STUDY (JAMES 2:14—4:12)

Read aloud James 2:14—4:12.

2:14–26 Faith and Works

In this passage, the author of the Letter of James presents a message that seems to contradict the stance of Paul the Apostle concerning work and faith. In Paul's Letter to the Romans, Paul writes that one who does not work, but who believes, is righteous, whereas James begins this passage in his letter saying that it does no good to say one has faith but does not have works. When viewed in the larger context of both passages, it is clear that Paul and the author of James are speaking from a different perspective. Both include Abraham as an example in their presentation, but it is a different aspect of Abraham's faith and works that each presents.

Paul the Apostle views works as works of the Mosaic Law that were central to Judaism. He stresses that Abraham pleased God because of his faith, before the law came into existence as it did later in history, during the time of Moses. Paul was challenging those who believed that righteousness comes to them through the practice of works of the Mosaic Law. He writes, "So also David declares the blessedness of the person to whom God credits righteousness apart from works" (Romans 4:6). In other words, David recognizes that the holiness of a person does not result from the practice of the works of the Mosaic Law, but from a person's faith.

Some Christians view James as contradicting Paul when he asks what good is it if one has faith without works. The difference between Paul and the author of James is that the author of James is not speaking about the works of the Mosaic Law or adhering to its commandments, but works in general such as charitable acts or a willingness to act selflessly based on faith in God. Following this view and using the example of Abraham as Paul did, he can state that the Lord justified Abraham because Abraham, through faith, was willing to perform the work of sacrificing his son, Isaac. Abraham believed, and his works proved his faith. For the author of James, it was the work of Abraham based on his faith that made him righteous.

The author expands on his message with examples. If a person encounters a brother or sister who has nothing to wear or eat and merely wishes him or her well without doing anything about it, what good is that? He repeats that faith without works is dead.

The author offers another challenge to those who claim to have faith without works. He asks them to show him faith without works, and he will show them his works as evidence of his faith. Through faith, a person can claim that God is one, but even demons can believe that God is one and tremble at the thought. He calls those people ignorant who do not recognize that Abraham's works proved his faith. It was his faith that led him to action. The author of James claims that this is why the Scriptures were fulfilled in Abraham, who believed in God, showed it by his works, and proved his righteousness.

Providing another image to prove his point, the author draws a lesson from Rahab, the prostitute. When the Israelites were planning to invade the Promised Land, they sent spies to reconnoiter the land, and Rahab helped them escape when they were threatened with capture. In return, they promised to protect Rahab against the Israelites when they invaded the country (see Joshua 2:1–21). The author of James views Rahab's protection of the spies as works that proved faith. The author ends by stating that faith without works is as dead as a body without a spirit.

3:1–12 Bridling the Tongue

The author begins this passage with a warning to aspiring teachers, that is, those who interpreted or shared messages with others. Some people were apparently establishing themselves as teachers, and the author reminds them that only a few are called to be teachers, since teachers, perhaps because of the importance of teaching within the community, can expect to be judged more strictly by the Lord.

The author then addresses the central theme of this section: the control of one's tongue. Aware that all of us make many mistakes in our lives, he states that those who control their speech reach perfection because they are, in fact, controlling their whole body. He uses two examples to demonstrate how something small can control something far larger. A bit in a horse's mouth controls the horse, and a rudder allows the helmsman to control a large ship, even in the midst of a gale. In the same way, a tongue is only a small member of the body, but it has great control.

Having made his point concerning the power of the tongue, the author turns his attention to the destruction that can be caused by a loose tongue. Just as a small spark or flame can set a whole forest on fire, so a loose tongue, like a tiny spark, can cause vast destruction. The author goes so far as to state that the tongue contains a whole world of iniquity in itself and can contaminate the whole body. The destructive flames of the tongue are with us from birth, and the tongue's flame has its source in hell. Here the author may be referring to the sinfulness that is seen as surrounding our human nature from the time of our birth.

The author continues to reflect on the power of the tongue. He is obviously speaking of the power of speech. While the human being can tame all the animals of the world, no one can tame the tongue. A person cannot be brought into subjection without controlling and disciplining the tongue, since the tongue speaks what the person thinks and wishes to say. The tongue looms as a restless evil, full of deadly poison. With the same tongue, we praise God and curse people who are made in the image of God. The author states that this contradiction should not exist, and he uses several images to emphasize his message. A spring doesn't pour out both fresh and salty water; olives do not come from fig trees, and salt water does not yield fresh water.

3:13–18 True Wisdom

In this passage, the author speaks of wisdom, which he understands as wisdom from God rather than the wisdom of this world. This wisdom from God is shown through acts of humility and a good life, while false wisdom leads to jealousy and self-seeking ambition. Such wisdom is a worldly wisdom and does not come from the Lord but from the earth. Those who claim such wisdom boast of nothing. They should not try to conceal the truth. False wisdom lacks spiritual roots and is evil. Where envy and selfish ambition exist, disorder and all kinds of wickedness exist. In contrast, wisdom from above is filled with virtue. True wisdom is pure, peaceable, gentle, considerate, and merciful, producing good deeds that are impartial and candid. Those who have sown in peace will produce a harvest of peace and righteousness.

4:1–12 Causes of Division

In contrast to peace, the author of James now speaks of the conflicts and battles that originate within the deepest desires of people. He asks where conflicts and wars within the community originate, and he answers that they come from the passions within people. These passions include coveting more than they possess, killing and living with envy without success, yet unable to obtain what they seek. They even fight and wage war. The reason they do not have what they desire is that they have not asked for it, or they have asked improperly, asking selfishly for something that indulges their own passions.

Addressing these people as "adulterers," the author asks whether they realize that friendship with the world makes them enemies of God. In the Old Testament, those referred to as adulterers were those who broke the covenant with God. Those who follow their passions and desires are the adulterers who abandon God. Like unfaithful spouses, they have given themselves to worldly desires.

The author questions whether the readers believe the Scriptures speak without meaning when they tell us the spirit made to dwell in us leads to jealousy. Since the author does not tell us the source of this Scripture reference and it is not found in known manuscripts, some commentators believe the author of James is quoting this passage from memory. This Scripture reference is difficult to understand. Some translate it differently, as though it is speaking of God's jealousy for the people of God. God looks into our hearts for a spirit of fidelity. In contrast to those who are God's enemies, those who are humble receive an abundance of grace from God (see Proverbs 3:34). The author urges his readers to submit themselves to God and to resist the devil who will, as a result, flee from them. As Christians draw nearer to God, God draws nearer to them.

The author urges Christians to wash their hands, a reference to cleansing evil from their lives. He urges those who are double-minded to purify their hearts, implying that they should seek the Lord instead of the world. Jesus once said a person cannot serve two masters, noting, "He will either hate one and love the other, or be devoted to one and despise the other" (Matthew 6:24).

Christians should discipline themselves, becoming aware of their wretched sins and weeping over them. He contrasts the evil pleasures of the world with the call for Christians to give themselves to God. They should discipline and mortify themselves so that their laughing turns to mourning and their joy turns into dejection. He is not telling Christians to live in the world as sullen, unhappy people, but as people who spiritually reject sinful, worldly pleasures. Christians are to humble themselves before the Lord who, in turn, will exalt them.

The author exhorts his readers not to speak evil of one another, and he compares slander against another or the judgment of another as equivalent to speaking evil against the law or judging the law. In speaking against the law, a person judges the law and is no longer a doer of the law. There is only one lawgiver and judge who is able to save and to destroy. The author does not name the Lord as the one judge and lawgiver, but it is obvious he is referring to the Lord. To attempt to take the place of the one lawgiver is to act against the law. The author challenges his readers, asking who they are to think they have the right to pass judgment on a neighbor. Since they are not the lawgivers, they do not have the right to judge their neighbor.

Review Questions

1. What does the author mean when he says that faith without works is dead?
2. Why is the author of the Letter of James so concerned about the use of the tongue in speaking?
3. What, according to the author, is true wisdom?
4. How does a lover of the world make himself or herself God's enemy?
5. What does the author mean when he tells readers to mourn and weep?

Closing Prayer (SEE PAGE 16)

Pray the closing prayer now or after *lectio divina*.

Lectio Divina (SEE PAGE 9)

Relax your body and maintain a posture of prayer (back straight, eyes shut, feet flat on the floor). This exercise can take as long as you want, but in the context of this Bible study, 10 to 20 minutes should be sufficient.

The meditations that follow are provided only to help group participants use this prayer form, but note that *lectio* is intended to bring one to a place of prayerful contemplation where the Word of God speaks to the hearer from his or her heart. (See page 9 for further instruction.)

Faith and Works (2:14–26)

A pastor spoke to a woman in his parish who claimed she had a difficult time feeling that God really existed and who believed she was losing her faith. The pastor knew the woman was a catechist, teaching in the parish religious-education program, and that she volunteered at the parish food pantry, but she still feared she lacked faith. The pastor asked why she volunteered to do all she did, and her answer was she believed it was important. If there were a God, she believed that this is what God would want her to do.

The pastor explained to her that her works proved she had faith. He added that faith was not a feeling but a dedication to God and proved she believed, even if she did not feel God's presence.

A short time later, the woman told her pastor she suddenly became aware she was trying too hard to believe. She said, "I believe my mother loves me, but she doesn't have to prove it by calling me every hour of the day. Even if I don't feel God's love or my mother's love, I know they love me. I decided to keep on doing what I'm doing for the love of such an elusive God."

Mother Teresa of Calcutta struggled with faith in God, but she never stopped serving the poor. She accepted the most difficult tasks because she believed feelings were not necessary for serving God, but good works were. The author of the Letter of James states that faith without works is dead, and our good works prove our faith.

✠ *What can we learn from this passage?*

Bridling the Tongue (3:1–12)

A woman told her confessor she gossiped too much and had a problem not talking about the weaknesses of others. The confessor, knowing the weather report called for March winds for the next several days, told her, as an act of satisfaction, to write the word "gossip" on a sheet of paper and tear it into twenty pieces. He directed her to go outside and throw the pieces of paper into the wind. Then she was to go and gather all the pieces of paper from the ground. He knew how difficult this would be and explained the reason for such an act was to show that gossip, once uttered, can rarely be retracted. Like the small pieces of paper, her words of gossip were irretrievably blowing in the wind for others to find.

The author of James compares the tongue to a small fire that can set a forest ablaze. In our modern world, the internet can become a type of communication like the tongue. For many people, gossip on the internet has caused overwhelming damage in their lives. There are many people who believe what they read on the internet to be true simply because it is on the internet. Destructive words, whether spoken or written, can ruin a person's reputation. The author reminds us we can use the tongue and other forms of communication to express our love of God or to destroy the lives of others.

✠ *What can I learn from this passage?*

True Wisdom (3:13–18)

A man, known to be skeptical about the good deeds and words of others, believed everyone was out for personal gain. His mantra in life was, "What's in it for me?" He believed everyone else thought this way. He claimed to be a realist about life and thought those who trusted others had an unrealistic and foolish view of life. Whenever someone pointed out his tendency toward skepticism he would answer it was not skepticism, but wisdom about the tendencies of human nature. Human beings, he claimed, always had hidden and selfish motives behind their actions.

The author of James would challenge this man's so-called wisdom. He would identify him as being false to the truth, ignoring his own tendencies toward jealousy or selfish ambition. Those with true wisdom do not act with skepticism toward the good deeds of others, but they act with the wisdom of the Lord. True wisdom recognizes the good in others and brings peace, mercy, and acceptance to others. Some people are ambitious and self-seeking, but many others are loving and kind. These latter show concern for others and possess true wisdom.

✠ *What can I learn from this passage?*

Causes of Division (4:1–12)

When Pope Francis made his first appearance as pope after his election, he greeted the crowd in a humble and loving manner that immediately electrified the crowd. He now held the highest office in the Roman Catholic Church, and he did not treat his office with pride or arrogance but with a sense of service and love. He expressed a concern for the poor, willing to mourn with them by entering into their suffering and need. He sought to live in as frugal and simple a manner as he could in this high office in the Church. This would be a hallmark of his pontificate.

The author of the Letter of James would identify with the attitude of Pope Francis. The author tells his readers not to love the world but to love God, speaking well of others and not judging them. He recognizes some people want to love God, but they love the world more. In doing this, they are people with two minds, one directed toward good and the other directed to the more powerful realm of the world. Pope Francis has one mind—love of God and neighbor. He shows no concern for worldly glory.

✠ *What can I learn from this passage?*

PART 2: INDIVIDUAL STUDY (JAMES 4:13—5)

Day 1: Warning Against Presumption (4:13–17)

The author of James challenges those who have made specific plans for trading and making profit, reminding them their life is like a mist that appears for a short time and disappears. In reality, they cannot plan for tomorrow. Instead of planning as if they have control of their own lives, they should always live with the idea they will perform their future deeds only if God wills it. Those who do not take God's will into account are boastful and arrogant, and—as such—are sinful. Because the author has continually been speaking about a person's manner of acting, he is consistent in stating anyone who knows what is right and does not do it commits sin.

Lectio Divina

Spend 8 to 10 minutes in silent contemplation of the following passage:

> A rich contractor in a small town where he was the only contractor often charged the people he served more for his services than an ordinary contractor would charge, and he used inferior materials in his buildings, sure that those who hired him would never discover how he cheated them. He told a friend who knew about his tactics that he intended to become an honest contractor after five years, once he secured enough funds to assure him and his family of a strong financial future. Since he considered himself a religious man, he intended to repent and live a good life when the five years ended. Unfortunately, he died unrepentant just short of his fifth year of work.

The author of James warns against such a presumptive way of thinking. He warns those who say, "Today or tomorrow I will make a profit with the hope of changing my ways," may not live until tomorrow. He warns that those, who know the right thing to do and omit doing it, commit a sin. Knowing death can overtake us at any moment, the author is saying we should not wait until tomorrow to live well but should start living close to the Lord today.

✠ *What can I learn from this passage?*

Day 2: Warning the Rich (5:1–6)

The author of James urges the rich to weep for the miseries they will be enduring. He is speaking of the judgment in store for those who glory in their wealth and he speaks as if the end were already taking place. Their wealth is rotting, their fine clothing is moth-eaten, their gold and silver corroded, and the corrosion will be a testimony against them. Unlike the faithful who have laid aside a glorious treasure for the last day, the treasure laid aside by the rich will be like a burning fire that will consume them. All the cheating they have done in their lives will cry out against them. The lost wages of the laborers and the cries of the harvesters will have "reached the ears of the Lord of hosts" (5:4).

In contrast to this judgment, the author reminds the rich they have lived a life of luxury and pleasure, fattened like animals for the day of slaughter. This day of slaughter is Judgment Day. The author tells the rich they are the ones who have condemned and murdered the righteous one, who offered them no resistance. The "righteous one" is not a reference to a particular person but to the poor who are unable to offer resistance.

When the author writes about the rich in this passage, he is placing his emphasis on those who are rich and cheat others. Their main concern is wealth, with little concern for God or others.

Lectio Divina

Spend 8 to 10 minutes in silent contemplation of the following passage:

A rich man, who was accustomed to people treating him with respect and deference, was growing old and had to have a leg amputated because of poor circulation. He sadly told a friend who was sitting by his bedside that all his wealth could not bring him good health. He was dying and, for the first time in his life, he was out of control of his destiny. Whatever he wanted in life, he could get.

Now, he felt like he was in prison and very much afraid to die. No matter how much money he had, he could not pay anyone to keep him from dying.

His friend became shocked when the once-powerful rich man began to cry. He wept, saying he was not accustomed to being so weak and unable to care for himself. He had it all, but he now realized he lacked the real necessities, namely the abilities to trust God and treat others with respect and dignity. He grabbed his friend's sleeve and cried out, "Don't let me die. I'm scared!"

Weeks later, when the friend stood before the rich man's casket, he remembered those last moments and recalled the words of Scripture that said all wealth is fleeting: "Vanity of vanities! All things are vanity!" (Ecclesiastes 1:2). The author of James warned that the cries of the workers cheated by the rich were crying out to the Lord. The days of luxury and oppression would end, and the person must come before the Lord. Jesus told a story about a rich fool who had such a bountiful harvest that he planned to build larger barns to store all his grain and other goods and live a life of luxury. But God said, "You fool, this night your life will be demanded of you; and the things you have prepared, to whom will they belong?" (Luke 12:20).

✠ *What can I learn from this passage?*

Day 3: Patience and Oaths (5:7–12)

Shortly after the resurrection of Christ, the people looked forward to his Second Coming, which they expected to occur soon. When the end did not come, they had to develop a new attitude toward the Second Coming. Central to this new attitude was the need to wait patiently and keep watch. The author begins this passage by urging his readers to be patient until the coming of the Lord. In urging his readers to be patient, he uses the image of a farmer who must wait through the autumn and spring rains before he can harvest his crops. In the same way, Christians are to remain patient and not grow weary, knowing at any moment the end could be at hand.

Some people, growing impatient, may begin to complain about one another, but the author warns them to avoid such grumbling so they will not be judged for it. The Judge, namely Jesus the Lord, is standing before the gates, ready to enter. In the Old Testament era, many of the towns were surrounded by walls into which homes were built. Gates were the only entrance to the town. The author of James pictures the Lord as standing in front of the gates, prepared to enter. This is meant to be an image of the last day.

In urging his readers to remain patient, the author chooses examples from the prophets of the Old Testament who spoke in the name of the Lord. Because of their endurance, these prophets are called blessed. The author recalls the perseverance of Job. By examining the life of Job, Christians are better able to understand God's purpose, knowing the Lord is compassionate and merciful.

The author adds an exhortation about swearing that actually has nothing to do with the preceding passage. He tells his readers not to swear by heaven or earth or use any oaths. Since the Letter of James is apparently written by a Christian Jew, he would naturally avoid using the sacred name of God in an oath, since Jews did not speak God's name. The author therefore speaks of not "swearing by heaven," in place of using the phrase "swearing by God."

The author reflects the message found in Matthew 5:33–37 concerning oaths. They should be so trustworthy that their "yes" and "no" are acceptable to others. If they cannot reach this stage of trustworthiness, then they will be liable to condemnation.

Lectio Divina

Spend 8 to 10 minutes in silent contemplation of the following passage:

Trust in the Lord takes patience. A preacher once told his assembly God always answers prayers. If we pray for a million dollars, God will answer our prayer one dollar at a time. We will receive our answer in God's good time, and in the meanwhile, we must be patient. In answering our prayer, God never says "no," but God says "yes...but be patient," or God says, "I have a better idea. Trust me!"

Praying and trusting God can take most of a person's life, but God is always answering the person's prayer in some manner. The story of St. Monica, who prayed most of her life for her son, Augustine, is an example of dedication and patient prayer. As a result of her prayers, Augustine not only converted to Christ but also became a major theologian in the Church and was canonized.

Patience is one of the major signs of trusting God. Just as the farmer must be patient while the seeds germinate and grow into a large crop, so we must be patient as our prayers germinate to the point where God produces the harvest for which we pray. The author of the Letter of James reminds us the Lord is compassionate and merciful. Keeping this in mind helps us to pray with perseverance and patience.

✠ *What can I learn from this passage?*

Day 4: The Power of Prayer (5:13–20)

The author of James strives to encourage his audience with a message about prayer in conflict. The one who is suffering should pray, while the one who is happy should sing songs of praise. The one who is sick should send for the "presbyters of the church," who in turn should pray over the sick person and anoint him or her in the name of the Lord. This concept originated in the early Jewish communities where the elders served as the leaders of the people. The presbyters in this passage serve a ministerial as well as a leadership role. Their prayers will save the sick persons, and the Lord will raise them up. More important to the early community was the forgiveness of sins, and the author reminds us that this forgiveness takes place through the prayers and anointing of the Church.

The author of James urges Christians to confess their sins to one another and to pray for one another in order to receive healing. The author declares that the prayer of the righteous is powerful and effective. As an example, he recalls Elijah, a human being like us, who prayed intensely that it would not rain, and it did not rain for three years and six months.

Rain returned only when Elijah prayed for it, thus allowing the land to bring forth the harvest. The author is reminding the community of the power of prayer. No one should think of himself or herself as powerless when it comes to prayer.

The author turns his attention to those who wander from the faith and the ministry of the community to one who is thus spiritually sick. He emphasizes the gifts given by God to the one who returns as well as to those who bring about the return. The sinner will be saved from spiritual death, and those who bring the sinner back will save their own souls and cover a multitude of sins, a statement that could include forgiveness for the sins of the community.

The Letter of James ends abruptly, which serves as another piece of evidence that the Letter of James was not a letter in the truest sense.

Lectio Divina

Spend 8 to 10 minutes in silent contemplation of the following passage:

A very ill woman was about to undergo a serious and dangerous operation. Her doctors assured her that as serious as the operation was, they had every reason to believe she would come through it successfully. When her pastor arrived to celebrate the sacrament of anointing of the sick, she became frightened. In catechism class, she learned that the anointing was known as the last rites, and she asked with some concern whether this meant she was dying. After her pastor assured her the Church anointed with words that prayed for healing and explained the sacrament, she relaxed.

In James, the author speaks of people summoning the presbyters (ordained priests) when people are sick, and presbyters are to pray over the sick, anoint them, and offer a prayer directed toward saving the sick and bring healing to them. The text tells us that if those who are ill have committed any sins, their sins will be forgiven.

✠ *What can I learn from this passage?*

Review Questions

1. Give examples of presumption in our life according to the thinking of the author?

2. What warning does the author give to those who are rich and oppress others?

3. Why does the author feel a need to speak of patience to his readers?

4. How do we use the author's words about anointing the sick in our sacrament of anointing today?

5. What is the reward for the person who brings a sinner back to the Lord?

A New People of God

1 PETER 1—5

Come to him, a living stone, rejected by human beings but chosen and precious in the sight of God, and, like living stones, let yourselves be built into a spiritual house to be a holy priesthood to offer spiritual sacrifices acceptable to God through Jesus Christ (2:4–5).

Opening Prayer (SEE PAGE 16)

Context

Part 1: 1 Peter 1—2 Many commentators view 1 Peter as a baptismal homily written to an audience of believers. The author, who is obviously not St. Peter but a later writer, alludes to various early hymns used in the baptismal liturgies of the day. Despite this evidence, there are some commentators who deny the letter is a type of baptismal homily.

Instead of using the Hebrew Old Testament as his source, the author of 1 Peter uses the Septuagint translation of the Old Testament that was a Greek translation of the Bible for those who spoke dominantly Greek and who lived outside Palestine. The author of 1 Peter writes flawless Greek, a fact that points to an author other than Peter, who was a Jew raised in an area of Palestine where Greek was rarely spoken and who was a fisherman who most likely had little education other than that which he may have received from the Hebrew-speaking religious teachers of his era. References in the letter to an extensive persecution of Christians point to a period after Peter was martyred (circa 64–67 AD).

The author addresses his letter to chosen sojourners in Asia Minor, who were sanctified through the blood of Christ, a reference to baptism. He praises the Lord, who gave his readers a new birth through the resurrection of Jesus Christ and urges them to rejoice, although they may suffer many trials for their faith. They will be tested as gold is tested by fire.

The author knows that his readers, although they have not seen the Lord, believe in him and love him. This belief leads to a series of moral exhortations concerning their manner of acting. Just as it was revealed to the prophets, they had the call to serve others, not themselves, and they should serve as obedient and holy children. They should conduct themselves with reverence and mutual love, ridding themselves of all malice and wickedness to become living stones to be built into a spiritual house of the Lord. They are to conduct themselves well so that people may see their good works and change their attitude toward them. As servants of the Lord, they should be obedient to civil leaders. Slaves should treat their masters with reverence, accepting discipline when it is deserved and accepting suffering in the spirit of Christ who suffered.

Part 2: 1 Peter 3—5 Christian spouses should treat each other with mutual love. The author speaks of wives as being submissive to their husbands and of husbands loving their wives as "joint heirs of the gift of life." No one is to return evil for evil or insult for insult. If they suffer for righteousness for the sake of Christ, they are blessed. They are to put to death the desires of the flesh as Jesus did and love one another, using the gifts given to them by Christ. They should not be surprised when they must suffer. They will be tested like gold in fire. Presbyters must tend to the flock of God, and other members of the community should be subject to the presbyters. They are to humble themselves before the Lord, trusting the Lord with one's cares. Be prepared always.

PART 1: GROUP STUDY (1 PETER 1—2)

Read aloud 1 Peter 1—2.

1:1–2 Greeting

The letter opens with the author identifying himself as "Peter, an apostle of Jesus Christ." In designating Peter as an apostle, the author could be referring to Peter as one of the original Twelve, in contrast to Paul, who declared he was "called to be an apostle" (Romans 1:1) by the risen Christ. Although Peter did not write the letter, the author uses his name since his authority among the apostles was known in the Church at the time the letter was written.

He sends his greetings to the "chosen sojourners of the dispersion" (1:1). The dispersion originally referred to those Israelite people who fled from Jerusalem at the time of the Babylonian invasion or at other periods when conquering armies appeared to threaten their land (see James 1:1). In 1 Peter, the new dispersion refers to Christian Gentiles. Because they are followers of Christ living among unbelievers, they are living as strangers in Asia Minor, Pontus, Galatia, Cappadocia, Asia, and Bithynia.

The author identifies these Gentile Christians as chosen or destined by God from the beginning. They were chosen by God the Father, made holy by the Spirit to be obedient to Jesus Christ and to be sprinkled with his blood. In the Book of Exodus, the people ratify their obedience to the covenant and Moses sprinkles blood on them, calling it "the blood of the covenant which the LORD has made with you" (Exodus 24:8). Through their baptism in the Spirit, the Christians in Asia Minor entered into a covenant with the Lord.

Although the names of God the Father, the Holy Spirit, and Christ are mentioned in this greeting, we cannot state the author is definitely alluding to the Trinity. "The Spirit" is often referred to as God's spirit, not in the sense of a person, but in the sense of God's power or movement. The usual prayer for grace and peace ends this greeting.

1:3–12 Praise of God

A thanksgiving usually follows the greeting. In 1 Peter, however, the thanksgiving takes the form of praising God, whom the author addresses as the "Father of our Lord Jesus Christ" (1:3). The author thanks God, who in his mercy has given us a new birth, which is a reference to baptism. In this passage, baptism gives us a living hope, namely a grace to be with us throughout our life. This birth (baptism) has its source in Jesus' resurrection from the dead and offers us an inheritance that remains pure and eternal.

In the Old Testament, the people of Israel were promised the inheritance of the land of Canaan, the Promised Land. Our inheritance is the eternal Promised Land, kept safe for us in heaven. Through faith, those who are to receive this inheritance are guarded with God's power until our salvation is revealed at the end of time.

Having already spoken of the hope possessed by Christians, the author calls this living hope for salvation a reason for rejoicing, even if Christians must face some temporary suffering in this earthly life. These trials test the genuineness of our faith, which is more precious than gold. For gold, even though it is ultimately perishable, is tested by fire. Everything of value is tested to establish its value. Tested faith will lead to the praise, glory, and honor of Jesus Christ.

The author tells his readers that although they have not seen Jesus, they still love him. The early Christians, unlike Peter, had not seen Christ, yet they loved him and experienced an indescribable joy because of their faith in him. The hope of achieving their goal of salvation was the reason for this joy.

The Old Testament prophets, still admired and honored by the people of the early Church, spoke about their search for the grace that was to come. The Holy Spirit spoke through these prophets of the suffering of Christ and the glories that would follow. The prophets sought the times and the circumstances surrounding these expectations, and they received revelations they knew were not for themselves but for future generations. In the Book of Isaiah, we read the Lord will exalt him (the Suffering Servant): "Because he surrendered himself to death, was counted among the transgressors, bore the sins of many, and interceded for the transgressors" (Isaiah 53:12). The author reminds his audience: They have received this good news of salvation through the prophets.

1:13–21 Ransomed by the Blood of Christ

The author of 1 Peter tells his readers to gird up the loins of their minds, which reminds the reader of the Israelites when they were celebrating the Passover before leaving Egypt. They ate "with [their] loins girt" (Exodus 12:11), ready for a journey. The author of 1 Peter tells his readers to have their minds set on a journey with the Lord. They are to dedicate their lives to the truths they have received in their conversion to Christ. They should constantly keep in mind the Second Coming of Christ and the hope this coming brings to them. When they were ignorant in the past, they had given in to sinful desires, but now, as Christians, they are called to be holy, as the one who calls them is holy. The author cites God's ancient call to his people as recorded in Leviticus 11:45: "You shall be holy, for I am holy."

As Christians journey through life, they must recall God shows no partiality when it comes to judging people's actions. Because they are pilgrims and strangers in a foreign land, which means they are away from their heavenly home, they must behave in a proper manner. The author reminds them they were ransomed from the useless way of life they received from their ancestors, not by gold and silver, but with the blood of Christ. This blood ransom is compared with the saving effects of the blood of the lamb as found in Israel's Passover celebration (see Leviticus 23:12).

Christ was chosen before the world began, but only in the present age—the age after the death and resurrection of Christ—was God's plan fully revealed. Many New Testament writers referred to the period after the death and resurrection of Christ as the end of the ages or the last day. The author states his readers have their faith through Jesus Christ. Through this faith, they are able to trust in God, who raised Jesus from the dead and glorified him so that Christians might have faith and hope.

1:22–25 Mutual Love for One Another

Christians are living in a new spiritual family that differs from the human family into which they were born. The author states they entered this new family through obedience to the truth (by initiation into the faith through baptism). Those who enter this family of love are people who sincerely love one another. The seed that produced this new birth for them was not a perishable, human seed but an imperishable seed that comes from the living and enduring Word of God.

The author then quotes from Isaiah stating all human flesh is like grass, and its glory is like that of the flowers of the fields: "The grass withers, and the flower wilts, but the word of our God stands forever" (Isaiah 40:6–8). That Word of God is the good news that Christians have received.

2:1–10 A Royal Priesthood, God's People

Since Christians dedicated themselves to the Lord, they must not practice any vices that are contrary to their new life as members of this new family. They should rid themselves of malice, guile, insincerity, envy, and slander. Now that they have a taste of the goodness of the Lord, the author urges them to be like newborn infants, longing for the pure, spiritual milk that enables them to work for their salvation. These words may imply that the Christians receiving this letter were new converts to the faith. They were not yet ready for the deeper truths of the faith and must first be nourished on simpler truths, just as babies are nourished on milk. This milk will help them grow into salvation, which is a life lived in accordance with this new birth.

The author urges his readers to come to Christ, the living stone who was rejected by the world but is most precious in God's eyes. The members of the Christian community, like living stones, are to allow themselves to be built into a spiritual house, to be a holy priesthood and—as such—are to offer spiritual sacrifices that are acceptable to God through Jesus Christ.

The author quotes from several Old Testament prophets, who speak of God's special concern for the Chosen People. In a passage from Isaiah the prophet, the Lord speaks of laying a precious and specially chosen cornerstone in Zion (Israel). Christians view the stone spoken of in this passage as referring to Jesus Christ. The faith of those who trust in him will never be shaken (see Isaiah 28:16).

For those with faith, this stone (Jesus Christ) is precious. In contrast, those without faith will never accept this stone. The author quotes from the Book of Psalms: "The stone the builders rejected has become the cornerstone" (Psalm 118:22). In 1 Peter, the builders refer to the Jews who rejected Christ. Jesus' death on the cross caused him to be an obstacle and a stumbling block, as Isaiah foretold (see Isaiah 8:14). It is the fate of those who do not believe in God's Word to stumble and fall.

The author declares those who believe in Christ are a new chosen race who can now claim all the gifts promised to the people of Israel. They are a royal priesthood, a holy nation, God's own people, chosen to proclaim the praises of God, who led them out of the darkness of their pagan lives into the Lord's marvelous light of faith. In the Book of Exodus, the Lord directs Moses to tell the people of Israel they are a "kingdom of priests, a holy nation" (Exodus 19:6). The author of 1 Peter views Christians as the new kingdom of priests and a holy nation. Since the Israelites viewed the Gentiles as lacking in faith in the one true God, they viewed them as living in spiritual darkness.

The author quotes from Hosea 1:9 and 2:25, saying once they were no people, but now they are God's Chosen People. In their pagan days, they received no mercy, but mercy is now given to them. Because of Christ, the living stone who was accepted by them but rejected by others, they now live a new life in Christ.

2:11–25 Maintaining Good Conduct

Because they are aliens and exiles in this world, the author reminds his readers to avoid all desires of the flesh that wage war on the soul. This attitude toward the world, however, should not permit them to forget they must give good examples to others, especially Gentiles. Even though these unbelievers will accuse the Christians of causing trouble, they (Christians) should behave in a blameless fashion. Gentiles, seeing them acting in this way, will have reason for giving glory to God on the day of the Second Coming. What they now denounce will become a source of praise for God.

Christians must not only act well toward Gentiles but they must also accept the social structures of the day. They must give obedience to every human institution. This includes obedience to the emperor, whom the author calls "supreme," and to his appointed governors, whose duty it is to punish criminals and reward the good. The author views this obedience to the social structure as God's will for Christians. In this way, they will silence their foolish opponents by their good behavior.

The author of 1 Peter, like the authors of the Pastoral Letters, is apparently concerned about the acceptance of Christians within the society in which they live. This acceptance includes the lives of slaves. The author is familiar with slavery and the suffering endured by slaves. Many of these slaves were educated people captured in wars. While some of them were fortunate enough to have kind masters, others had harsh and unfair masters. The author urges all Christian slaves, regardless of their treatment, to show respect and obedience to their masters. As in other New Testament letters that speak of slavery, the author of 1 Peter does not challenge the existing social structure.

The author reminds slaves that while it is possible for them to gain merit by accepting undeserved suffering, there is no merit in accepting the suffering they deserved. The merit comes through accepting undeserved suffering patiently, even after the slaves have performed their duty well.

As an example of patient suffering, the author urges the slaves to consider Jesus Christ's suffering. He applies a passage from Isaiah's songs of the Suffering Servant to Christ, who committed no sin, spoke without deceit, accepted insult without insulting in return, made no threats when tortured, and put his trust in God, the just judge (see Isaiah 53:5–12). Christ took the sins of all on himself and, in his crucifixion, he died to sin so that all of us, dead to sin with him, could be raised to a new life in union with him.

The author tells his readers they were healed by Christ's wounds. Christ did all this, not for the people who were loyal and deserved it, but for the straying sheep. The author continually reminds his readers of their previous life as unbelieving pagans. Now, as believing Christians, they return to the shepherd and guardian of their souls like sheep who have strayed. In this way, Christ offers them an example for their suffering and serves as their protector in the midst of torment.

Review Questions

1. What does the author mean when he addresses his letter to sojourners of the dispersion?
2. Although the author never mentions baptism, how does he refer to the source of the sacrament of baptism and its effect on us?
3. Why does the author say the prophets of old received revelations which were not for them, but for future generations?
4. What does the author mean when he speaks of girding the loins of one's mind?
5. What motive does the author give for loving one another?
6. How can Christians be living stones built into a spiritual house?
7. How should Christians respond to civil authority?
8. How is Christ a model of obedience for slaves?

Closing Prayer (SEE PAGE 16)

Pray the closing prayer now or after *lectio divina*.

Lectio Divina (SEE PAGE 9)

Relax your body and maintain a posture of prayer (back straight, eyes shut, feet flat on the floor). This exercise can take as long as you want, but in the context of this Bible study, 10 to 20 minutes should be sufficient.

The meditations that follow are provided only to help group participants use this prayer form, but note that *lectio* is intended to bring one to a place of prayerful contemplation where the Word of God speaks to the hearer from his or her heart. (See page 9 for further instruction.)

Greeting (1:1–2)

In San Salvador, when the government was persecuting the peasants, one of the peasant catechists encouraged other suffering peasants to recognize the role of baptism in their life. He emphasized that when they were baptized into Christ, they were baptized into his blood. His preaching about Christ and baptism made him extremely popular among the peasants. One morning, his adult son found his father's slain body in an alley behind his father's house. In the middle of the previous night, a small government force entered the village, dragged the catechist from his home, and killed him. They feared he was becoming too powerful and could incite a rebellion against the government. His message, however, emphasized peaceful reform, not bloodshed.

In 1 Peter, the author speaks of being sprinkled with the blood of Jesus Christ, which is a reference to baptism. This is the message taught by the catechist. All of us who accept baptism are also called to live and die for Christ. This means we should be prepared to face martyrdom for Christ if necessary, or it could mean we must be willing to live for Christ, enduring insult, ridicule, rejection, and worldly temptations that would lead us away from Christ. Each time we share in the eucharistic celebration, we are renewing our baptismal call to live a life dedicated to Christ, who suffered and died that we may have life.

✠ *What can I learn from this passage?*

Praise of God (1:3–12)

A man visited his elderly aunt, who was suffering greatly and was near death. A slight movement of her body would cause her to cry out in pain. The man told his aunt he was having a difficult time praising a God who allowed such suffering in the world. The aunt, in the midst of her pain, answered she believed her acceptance of the intense pain was a gift from God, and God was preparing a special place for her because of trust in God at this time.

When the author of 1 Peter speaks of the pain some people must endure, he compares it to gold tested by fire. He states this acceptance of pain and trust in God leads to the praise, glory, and honor of God. It is not that God directly wills this suffering, but God recognizes the extreme faith the woman and others like her show in remaining faithful to loving God at such a time.

✠ *What can I learn from this passage?*

Ransomed by the Blood of Christ (1:13–21)

Saint Teresa of Ávila endured many hardships in her life, but she always remained faithful to the Lord. She considered her life to be a journey, saying we should realize the Lord is on our journey with us. The author of 1 Peter reminds us to conduct ourselves with reverence during our sojourn through life. The Lord was willing to suffer and die to bring us to salvation.

Following the directives of St. Teresa of Ávila, who was deeply conscious of all Jesus did for us and who trusted God's immense love, we should realize we are not walking through this world alone. Christ, who is God from all eternity and who gave himself for us, is on the journey with us. When we reflect on God's great love as shown through the life, death, and resurrection of Christ, we, like St. Teresa, can develop a consciousness of God's presence among us. With faith in Christ, we never walk through this life alone.

✠ *What can I learn from this passage?*

Mutual Love for One Another (1:22–25)

It is reported that St. Augustine once said, "Love God and do what you want." He believed a person who truly loves God cannot be satisfied with anything less than loving God. The love of God becomes the driving force for the person's life. It leads to love of neighbor, and love of one's neighbor leads back to love of God. Those who truly love the Lord cannot perform an action contrary to that love.

In 1 Peter, the author calls readers to love one another. This is also Jesus' message, namely we should love our neighbor. All that Jesus commanded never changes. Life will end, but God's Word (uttered by Jesus) will never pass away.

✠ *What can I learn from this passage?*

A Royal Priesthood, God's People (2:1–10)

During a Sunday homily, a preacher referred to Teresa of Ávila, who said humility is truth. The truth is we are important to God, and God gave us special talents, gifts, faith, and missions in life that creation needs. We are extremely important and worthwhile. God created us, and God does not make mistakes. We can admit we have gifts, but we must recognize our gifts come from God for the common good, and God can deprive us of these gifts at any moment.

The author of 1 Peter tells us how important and good we are. His message lies at the root of our faith. He declares Jesus is a living stone rejected by the builders, and we are living stones built into a spiritual house (the body of Christ) to be a holy priesthood. All the baptized belong to the household of God. According to the author of 1 Peter, we are a chosen people, a royal priesthood, a holy nation, a people of God. What more could be said about our dignity?

✠ *What can I learn from this passage?*

2:11–25 Maintaining Good Conduct

When Thomas More refused to proclaim Henry VIII as the head of the Church of England, he declared he was the king's loyal servant but God's first. He was a loyal friend to the king during many years of his life when he served the king, and he obeyed the wishes of the king until the king declared himself the head of the Church of England. More could not accept this rule and was beheaded because some viewed his refusal to accept that Henry VIII was the head of the Church as an act of treason. News of his death traveled rapidly throughout Europe, and many could hardly believe Henry VIII had his once-loyal servant and friend beheaded.

Thomas More followed the same principles presented in 1 Peter by remaining obedient to lawful authority as the will of God. He was faithful to Henry VIII until Henry sought a spiritual authority that More believed was an affront against God. He realized that he was a sojourner on this earth, subject to the king but subject to God first.

✠ *What can I learn from this passage?*

PART 2: INDIVIDUAL STUDY (1 PETER 3—5)

Day 1: Christian Conduct (3:1–12)

In this passage, the author speaks of the duties of husbands and wives, devoting most of his attention to an explanation of how Christian wives should act. During the era when 1 Peter was written, the husband was considered the head of the household. If he became a Christian, it was presumed his wife and the whole household would become Christian as well. On the other hand, when a wife became Christian, her husband did not necessarily follow her into Christianity. In such cases, the author tells these Christian wives how to behave with their non-Christian husbands.

The author begins by stating wives should be obedient to their husbands, a simple instruction based on the common thinking of the day. The motive behind the wife's obedience, however, is the Christian motive of setting a good example so husbands, who have refused to listen to the Gospel message, will choose to become Christian.

Recognizing a person's true worth and adornment lies within a person, the author instructs wives they should avoid all earthly fashions and adornment such as braiding their hair, wearing jewelry, or dressing in fine clothing. A gentle and quiet disposition provides lasting beauty and is a precious adornment in God's eyes. The author views this manner of acting as the way the holy women of the past adorned themselves. They trusted in God and accepted they were subordinate to their husbands.

The author uses Sarah, Abraham's wife, as an example of a trusting and obedient wife She called her husband her "lord." Finally, the author tells those wives who read his message that they are true children of Sarah when they do what is good and do not succumb to fear.

The passage indicates that in some areas, during the period of the early Church, the cultural position of women was equivalent to that of slaves. Since the woman belonged to her husband, she owed him obedience. Just as a master possessed his slave, so a man possessed his wife.

In the single verse of this letter that pertains to the duty of husbands, the author makes a radical statement for his day, telling husbands they must also realize their wives are equal heirs to God's grace. They should be understanding and honor women. If husbands act with these motives, then nothing will hinder their prayers from being answered. In reading about the role of women and men in the society in which the author wrote, we must realize their views reflect the culture in which they lived, and they are not presenting a theological view when speaking of women being subordinate to men.

The author deals with the total attitude Christians should possess toward others. They should develop a single-mindedness that demands they understand each other, love one another, and be compassionate and humble. They should not respond hurtfully to others who hurt them, not repaying evil for evil or insult for insult. They should instead return a blessing when hurt and, in doing this, inherit a blessing for themselves.

The author adapts Psalm 34:13–17 to his message and freely uses it to tell his readers that those who wish to enjoy a prosperous life must keep their tongues from evil and their lips from deceit. They must never turn to evil but must practice goodness, seeking for and pursuing peace. In doing this, they will receive favor from the Lord, who has eyes for those who are virtuous and ears to hear their cry. The Lord frowns on those who are evil.

Lectio Divina

Spend 8 to 10 minutes in silent contemplation of the following passage:

A man who worked at a large grocery mart would become angry with some of the demands made by his customers, but despite his anger, he would greet them with a smile and act as though he were genuinely concerned about them. His difficulty with people was spilling over into his home life, where he often argued with and insulted his wife and children.

Recognizing the turmoil he was causing at home because of his job, he sought help from his pastor. After listening to the man's troubles, the pastor told him to reflect on the passage in 1 Peter where the author teaches that everyone should be of one mind, loving and compassionate toward one another. The man reluctantly agreed, believing that meditating on this solution to his problem would not help.

Each day during the following week, the man meditated on 1 Peter until one day he suddenly realized the author was not only speaking about his relationship with his customers but also with his family. In their arguments, he would be less careful and more cutting and hurtful. He did not feel a need to be as kind to them as he was to his customers.

In 1 Peter, the man read we should not return evil for evil or insult for insult. He suddenly recognized his impatience with his customers was leading to impatience with his family. He resolved to solve his problem by meditating on patience and never exchanging hurt for hurt or insult for insult. He hoped his patience with his customers would lead to patience with his family, which it did. Saint Augustine once said patience is the companion of wisdom.

✠ *What can I learn from this passage?*

Day 2: Christian Suffering (3:13–22)

The author tells his readers that those committed to doing what is right cannot be harmed by anyone. If they must suffer for doing what is right, they will be blessed. He tells them they have no need to fear or to worry about those who would try to hurt them, but instead should honor Christ as the Lord in their hearts. For those who ask the reason for their hope in Christ the Lord, Christians should be prepared to offer an explanation of their faith and hope, sharing it with gentleness and respect for the person who questions them.

Christians who practice good behavior are called to live with a clear conscience. Those who speak falsely against them for their faithful life in Christ will be put to shame. If it is God's will they should suffer, then it is better to suffer for doing good than for doing evil.

In the following passage, the author summarizes a variety of truths relating to Christ and suffering. He recalls Christ died for sins once and for all. This death of Jesus need not be repeated, since the act of atonement on Jesus' part was complete in itself. Christ was innocent, yet he died for those who were not innocent. He was the righteous one dying for the unrighteous. The purpose of his death was to lead all people to God, yet the story doesn't end with Jesus' death. The author witnesses to the resurrection of Jesus, stating he was "put to death in the flesh" and "brought to life in the spirit."

The author adds that Christ, in the spirit, visited and preached to the spirits in prison. The passage does not clearly identify for us who "the spirits in prison" are. The message is: Christ really died, and by his death and resurrection, he conquered all evil.

The author draws a parallel with the days of Noah. At that time, many people were disobedient, but God waited patiently for the ark to be built. When it was ready, God saved eight people in the ark. Instead of seeing the waters of the Flood as destructive, the author sees them as a sign of salvation for those saved from spiritual death. The waters prefigured the waters of baptism that offer us salvation. These waters do not wash away physical stain but stand as a pledge of a new life in God through Christ's resurrection. In his glory, Jesus Christ went to heaven and holds the place of honor at God's right hand. In ancient times, the honored position was at the right hand of the king, and it often signified a power akin to that of the king. All the angels, authorities, and powers of heaven are subject to Jesus Christ.

Lectio Divina

Spend 8 to 10 minutes in silent contemplation of the following passage:

A nun who was dying often found herself in pain when she lay in one position for a long period of time. Every fifteen minutes, a nurse would come to her room in the infirmary to reposition a pillow under the knees or help roll her on her side. One day, a woman came to the visit the nun. The woman was having family problems and needed to speak with someone. Knowing the nun had the reputation of being a skilled listener, the woman spoke with her for a little more than an hour. Whenever the nurse came to move the nun, she would simply say, "Not now."

When the woman visiting the nun finally left, the nun was in such pain that she could hardly speak. She said to the nurse, "Please reposition the pillow under my knees." The astonished nurse realized the nun must have been in pain throughout most of the woman's visit, and she asked why the nun did not make this request earlier.

The nun answered, "This poor woman was suffering from her ordeal. My pain did not matter. It was such a small pain compared to Jesus' suffering on the cross." Saint Maximilian Kolbe, who accepted starvation and great pain in place of another prisoner in a concentration camp, once said he was willing to suffer more for Jesus Christ. Saints did not seek suffering, but they were willing to accept it when it came.

✠ *What can I learn from this passage?*

Day 3: Christian Charity (4:1–11)

The author exhorts his readers to recall that Christ suffered in this life, and they are called to suffer with the same attitude of Christ. This suffering is not simply random suffering that occurs in every person's life, but the suffering encountered by the one who has chosen the way of Christ over the way of evil. Through the rite of baptism, a person enters this suffering in union with Christ. The author urges the baptized to spend the remainder of their lives fulfilling the will of God. He reminds them they have already spent enough time on sinful practices, saying enough time has passed for them to do what the pagan Gentiles do. Using a common list of vices, the author identifies these sinful activities in which they once lived as licentiousness, evil passions, drunkenness, orgies, carousing, and lawless idolatry.

When Christians no longer live such an evil life, their pagan companions are surprised, and they will spread slander about the Christian converts. The author of the letter dramatically views the sinners as plunging themselves into a swamp of sinfulness. Just as those who have turned to Christ will give an accounting of their lives on the Day of Judgment, so will those who continue to live as pagans. The author explains that Christians, even those who have died, will overcome the condemnation of sin (living in the flesh) and "live in the spirit." The author realizes pagans may seem to be hopelessly condemned, but he notes they still have a chance to change their lives.

Some in the early Church believed that since the first coming of Christ into the world took place, the Second Coming would happen soon. Following this manner of thinking, the author tells his readers the end is at hand, and they must prepare themselves by living virtuous lives. He urges them to remain serious and disciplined so they can pray better.

A life of virtue includes life in the community and should consist of a firm love for one another, "because love covers a multitude of sins" (4:8). The parallel expression concerning love covering sins is also in the Book of Proverbs where the author of the book writes, "Hatred stirs up disputes, but love covers all offenses" (Proverbs 10:12). Christians should be hospitable to one another without complaining.

As stewards of God's gifts, Christians should share their specific gift with others. The one with the gift of preaching should faithfully preach the Word of God; the one with the gift of serving should serve in accordance with the strength given by God. By their proper use of these gifts, they will be praising God through Jesus Christ. The author concludes with an acclamation of praise and honor to God: "to whom belong the glory and dominion forever and ever. Amen."

Some commentators believe this portion of the letter ends a baptismal liturgy used by the early Church. The passage ends with the prayer of praise to God, and it adds an "Amen" to the end of the prayer. Although the "Amen" is found as a spontaneous prayer in the middle of letters, it was also used as an end to prayer, in the same way we use it today.

Lectio Divina

Spend 8 to 10 minutes in silent contemplation of the following passage:

A surprising number of saints rejected wealth to become dedicated followers of Christ. Saint Francis of Assisi came from a wealthy family and rejected his wealth to don a beggar's robe and live in extreme poverty. Saint Ignatius of Loyola and St. Francis De Sales both came from wealth but rejected it to follow Christ. These saints rejected the flesh and pleasures of a wealthy life in the world to follow Christ. Because they abandoned their riches and became dedicated followers of Jesus Christ, we know their outstanding place in history. If they had retained their wealth, we may never have heard of them.

The author of 2 Peter urges his readers to follow the example of Jesus Christ and reject a life centered on gratifying the flesh. The Lord has given us all gifts and wishes us to use these gifts for proclaiming his message to the world, using our words as well as our example of Christian living.

There are some who are wealthy who are using their wealth for the good of others. Jesus' message means we live in the world and can enjoy many of the gifts found in God's creation, but central to one's life is service to Christ over all else. Some saints have abandoned their wealth, and others have used their wealth for the good of society. There is more than one way to become a saint in God's creation.

✠ *What can we learn from this passage?*

Day 4: Trial by Fire (4:12—5)

The author now speaks as if the people were already enduring some type of suffering. He had spoken earlier about the trials to be expected by Christians, and how they are to be tested by fire in the same way gold is tested (see 1 Peter 1:6–7). He now states they should not be surprised this trial is taking place. For people of faith, sharing in the sufferings of Christ is a cause for joy because of the great gift that will be given to them at the time of the Second Coming, the time when the glory of Christ will be revealed. Those who are insulted for the name of Christ are blessed (happy) because the spirit of glory, which is the spirit of God, is with them.

The author calls his readers to be open to suffering for good rather than for evil. He states no one should "be made to suffer as a murderer, a thief, a criminal, an evildoer," which would be shameful. Christians, however, should find no shame in suffering because they are Christ's followers, and should offer thanks and praise to God because of the name Christian.

The author implies the judgment will begin with the Church because its members have received so many gifts. Adapting from the Book of Proverbs, the author states if the judgment is so strict for those who are the followers of Christ, how much more strict will it be for those who refuse to accept the Gospel message (see Proverbs 11:31)? For this reason, those whom God allows to suffer should continue to perform good deeds and entrust themselves to the faithful Creator.

The author addresses the officially appointed leaders within the community, the presbyters. The author speaks of himself as a fellow presbyter and states he speaks from the authority of one who was a witness to the sufferings of Jesus Christ. The author's identification here may refer to the idea that he personally witnessed the passion and death of Christ (as Peter did), or it could mean he suffered as Jesus suffered, and his own suffering for Christ was a witness to the world of the unity of Christ's suffering with Christians. The author believes he will share in the "glory to be revealed" when Jesus returns. By identifying himself as a presbyter, a witness to Christ's suffering, and one who expects glory on the last day, the author has established his authority to make an appeal to other presbyters.

The role of the presbyters is to carefully shepherd the flock as Christ did. They can do this by willingly serving with generosity and not for disgraceful recompense, and leading by example rather than domineering the flock. In so doing, the presbyters will receive the eternal crown of glory when Christ, the chief shepherd, appears.

The author turns his attention to the younger members, urging them to follow the teachings of the presbyters and adding they should act with humility when dealing with one another. Quoting from the Book of Proverbs, the author reminds them God scoffs at the proud and favors the humble (see Proverbs 3:34).

The author urges the young men to remain humble under the powerful hand of God so God may exalt them in due time. Because of God's continual care for them, they should place their concerns in the hands of the Lord.

In typical fashion when speaking of the end times, the author encourages his readers to discipline themselves and to stay alert, to resist the devil that prowls "like a roaring lion looking for someone to devour." The author urges his readers to keep in mind that other Christian believers throughout the world are enduring similar sufferings, adding for the comfort of his readers that they will not have to suffer long, and God will restore, strengthen, and support them. He ends with a spontaneous acclamation by praying that dominion will be the Lord's forever.

A common practice of the day was to use secretaries who were trained in letter writing. Silvanus is named as the writer or secretary through whom this letter was written. This may account for the excellent Greek found in the letter. The author tells us he trusts Silvanus as one who is concerned about other Christians, and he claims he sent this letter to encourage his readers never to abandon the true grace of God to which he witnesses in these words.

He then sends greetings from the Church in Babylon, which is the name used in the Book of Revelation when referring to Rome. The Jewish people remembered ancient Babylon as a place of sin, a horrendous place where their ancestors lived in captivity for about half a century. Rome is the new Babylon. The author sends greetings from Mark, who could be Mark the evangelist or another companion with the same name. The Book of the Acts of the Apostles states that Peter, who was released from prison by an angel, "went to the house of Mary, the mother of John, who is called Mark" (Acts 12:12). Mark later becomes a companion of Paul the Apostle on his missionary journeys (see Colossians 4:10)

He directs them to offer one another a loving kiss, which was the gesture of unity in Christ shared among Christians. He wishes peace to all who are in Christ.

Lectio Divina

Spend 8 to 10 minutes in silent contemplation of the following passage:

In 1980, four missionaries who worked with the poor in San Salvador were killed after they left the country's major airport by members of the Salvadoran army. The missionaries consisted of two Maryknoll sisters named Maura Clark and Ita Ford, an Ursuline sister named Dorothy Kazel, and a lay missionary named Jean Donovan. When the soldiers who were supposed to be escorting them from the airport turned down a dirt road, they had to realize that they would soon be facing torture, rape, and death.

When the four missionaries agreed to work among the poor in San Salvador, they must have realized the dangers they faced, but their courageous faith overcame their fears. In the Gospel of John, Jesus warned his disciples they could encounter rejection and even death for love of him. He told them, "If the world hates you, realize that it hated me first" (John 15:18). He added, "If they persecuted me, they will also persecute you" (John 15:20). The author of 1 Peter follows a similar theme, saying whoever is made to suffer for Christ should realize it is for the glory of Christ.

All in the community—presbyters and the laity—have a call to witness to the suffering of Christ. The four missionaries in San Salvador witnessed to Christ by their concern for the poor and their death at the hands of the Salvadorian military. Their faith fulfilled the prophecy of Jesus Christ; they would be killed for his sake. In the early Church, many Christians viewed dying for Christ to be a gift from God.

✠ *What can I learn from this passage?*

Review Questions

1. What does the author of 1 Peter mean when he speaks of wives being subordinate to their husbands?
2. What is the understanding of the author of 1 Peter when he speaks of living with one mind?
3. How should Christians respond to suffering?
4. Why is being hospitable important?
5. Should Christians expect to be persecuted?
6. How should presbyters act?
7. What does the author of 1 Peter say about trusting God in times of temptation?

True Knowledge of Christ

2 PETER 1–3

Know this first of all, that there is no prophecy of Scripture that is a matter of personal interpretation, for no prophecy ever came through human will; but rather, human beings moved by the holy Spirit spoke under the influence of God (1:20–21).

Opening Prayer (SEE PAGE 16)

Context

Part 1: 2 Peter 1—2 Since the author of 2 Peter possessed a knowledge of many New Testament writings and was familiar with the Gospel accounts of the transfiguration, 1 Peter, and the collected letters of Paul, commentators believe 2 Peter was written at a late date by an anonymous author using Peter's name. This letter sought to correct a growing doubt about the Second Coming of Christ and to offset the preaching of false teachers. Except for the opening greeting, 2 Peter lacks many of the components of a true letter.

Although the author of 2 Peter is not Peter, he identifies himself as "Symeon Peter, a slave and apostle of Jesus Christ" (1:1). In early Church writings, the greeting would often begin with the writer identifying himself as a servant, or slave, of the Lord Jesus Christ and as an apostle. Both the title of a slave and an apostle had become acceptable titles for those chosen to preach the Gospel message.

The author of 2 Peter knows the people he is addressing are challenged by a number of false teachings, and he intends to offer them true knowledge concerning God and Jesus Christ. In his letter, he reminds his readers they have received promises and gifts that offer them a share in the divine nature. He urges them to reinforce their faith with the practice of virtue, which leads to knowledge and mutual love and enables them to actively live in union with Jesus Christ. By practicing virtue, they will have the assurance of entry into the eternal kingdom.

The intention of the author in writing his letter is to continually remind his readers of the message of faith that they already possess. He claims he taught them true doctrine about Jesus Christ, devoid of all myths, a message he heard when the voice from heaven declared Jesus was the Son of God. He warns against false prophets in their midst who will deny all that Christ, the Master, has taught them. He reminds them that throughout history, there were false prophets who faced obliteration. He recalls God's destruction of sinners in the days of Noah and Sodom and Gomorrah and how God saved Noah, Lot, and their families from destruction. He warns that in denouncing the Lord, they would be bringing destruction on themselves.

Part 2: 2 Peter 3 Some people were denying the Second Coming of Christ, scoffing at those who believe Christ will come again. They view the delay in Christ's coming as a sign the Second Coming will not take place. The author of 2 Peter points out a thousand years are like a day to the Lord, and instead of viewing the Second Coming as being delayed, they should view the delay as a sign of God's patience in allowing people time to repent. He exhorts his readers to be prepared for this final day. He ends with a further call for the people to gain true knowledge of Jesus Christ.

PART 1: GROUP STUDY (2 PETER 1—2)

Read aloud 2 Peter 1—2.

1:1–11 Living With Spiritual Knowledge

As the author does in 1 Peter, the writer of 2 Peter identifies himself as an apostle of Jesus Christ, basing his authority on the call to be an apostle by Jesus during his lifetime on earth. Although the author is not Peter, he writes, as the author of 1 Peter does, from the viewpoint of the leader of the apostles. In 2 Peter, he adds that he is a slave of Jesus Christ, an opening found also in letters of Paul. Paul, for instance, begins his Letter to the Romans by identifying himself as "a slave of Christ Jesus" (Romans 1:1).

The author of 2 Peter addresses those who have received a faith equal to that of Peter. They receive this gift "through the righteousness of our God and savior Jesus Christ" (1:1). The author prays his readers will be filled with grace and peace in abundance as their knowledge of God and of Jesus the Lord grows. He recognizes his readers are facing challenges to their faith in the form of false messages concerning God and Jesus.

The author speaks about the gifts given by God through Christ and the response of Christians to these gifts. He teaches it is through the divine power of the Lord that we have received all the gifts we need for living a truly devout life. These gifts enable us to know God, who has called us through the power and glory of Christ. In receiving these gifts, we received a pledge of something to come that will be both great and precious. Christians become capable of sharing in the divine nature and escape from the corruption of evil desires encountered in the world.

The author of 2 Peter addresses the proper use of these gifts. Because of all the gifts Christians have received, they must strive to grow in faith by building one virtue on another. They should build faith on their practice of virtue, virtue on knowledge, knowledge on self-control, self-control on endurance, endurance on godliness, godliness on mutual affection, and mutual affection on love. These gifts make a person effective and productive and will lead to a true knowledge of the Lord Jesus Christ.

Without these gifts, people become so shortsighted they are nearly blind, forgetting they have been cleansed of their past sins.

Reminding Christians of their special call, the author urges his readers to work harder to make their call firm and permanent. In doing so, they will be rewarded with entry into the eternal kingdom of our Lord and Savior Jesus Christ.

1:12–21 Apostolic Witness

Because of the importance of his message, the author believes he must continually repeat the truth, even when his readers show evidence of knowing and following his message faithfully. He feels he must continue to remind them of Christ's message while he is still in "this 'tent,'" which is a reference to the body (1:13). The Apostle Paul also applies the image of a tent to a body, comparing our life in the body as an earthly tent which will be destroyed for the sake of an eternal dwelling (see 2 Corinthians 5:1–5).

When the author of 2 Peter declares he will soon put this tent aside, he appears to be speaking of his impending death. This gives his message a sense of urgency, as though it were a last will and testament. He refers to this message about his tent as coming from the Lord, saying the Lord Jesus Christ has shown this message to him. He informs his readers he will make every effort to enable them to recall all the elements of the message he has preached, even after his death. This could be a reference to the letter he is writing to instruct them.

The author then speaks against those who deny the Second Coming of Christ and who reinterpret the Scriptures on their own. He does not make use of shrewdly contrived myths to convince them of the truth he teaches as the false teachers do. Instead, he declares he personally witnessed the honor and glory Christ received from God the Father. He heard the voice of God, who majestically proclaimed, "This is my beloved Son, with whom I am well pleased." This is a reference to the transfiguration of Christ, which Peter witnessed along with James and John, "while we were with him on the holy mountain" (see Matthew 17:1–8).

As a witness to the transfiguration, the author, speaking as though he were Peter, states this is a reliable prophetic message, and that his readers should follow it like a lamp shining in a dark place, trusting it until dawn arrives. This prophetic message should guide them through the darkness of this world until the day when everything is seen in the light of God's glory.

Just as prophecy enables a person to speak about God through the power of the Holy Spirit, so the one who interprets prophecy must also possess this presence of the Spirit. Although the Lord uses human beings as instruments for revealing prophecy, they are truly instruments of the Holy Spirit, prophesying under the inspiration of God. Interpretation of Scripture is not a matter of personal initiative but of God's initiative. The author's exhortation here appears to condemn those who use shrewdly contrived myths to teach falsehood.

2 False Teachers

Reminding his readers of the false prophets of the past, in chapter 2 the author warns false prophets exist even now as they did in previous centuries. The false prophets of the author's day are those who teach their own heretical views and deny in practice the Master who purchased their freedom by his life. "Master" refers to Jesus Christ.

In an attempt to win followers for themselves, these prophets will try to deceive them with cunning words. In denying the Master, they bring destruction on themselves. They will have many followers who will accept their wicked ways, causing the truth to become detested. They will exploit the followers of Christ with falsehoods, but from long ago they were already condemned and their obliteration was always present.

The author of 2 Peter points to the angels, stating God did not spare them when they sinned, even they were condemned to the depths of darkness until the Day of Judgment.

He then draws examples from the Book of Genesis. In the time of Noah, God destroyed all the people in the Flood except Noah, who was righteous, and seven others: his wife, three sons, and their wives (see Genesis 6:5—7:24). The people of Sodom and Gomorrah were destroyed in ashes as a warning for future generations. God saved Lot, another righteous man, who was sickened by the sin that surrounded him, and he rejected it (see Genesis 19:1–29). The author uses these examples to show the Lord, while saving those who are just, continues to punish sinful people until the Day of Judgment. This does not mean the condemned will no longer suffer punishment after this day, but it is the day when all will come to their eternal judgment. The author tells his readers the Lord knows how to treat those who live only for their own corrupt desires and who lack respect for authority.

The author states the false prophets are so bold and haughty that they have no fear of berating heavenly creatures such as angels. The angels, despite their greater power, do not bring against them a judgment of condemnation from the Lord. These false prophets, ridiculing those things they do not understand, act on instinct like ignorant animals destined by nature to be caught and destroyed. Because they are depraved, they will destroy themselves and receive the reward of the wicked.

The author views these false prophets as blotches on society who waste their lives and prey on those with whom they revel. He sees them as luring weak people into sexual sins, as adulterers with a voracious appetite for sin and filled with greed. Because of their sinfulness, they live under a curse, following the same path as Balaam, a false prophet of the Old Testament. The author is referring to a story in the Book of Numbers that tells of the prophet Balaam being hired to curse the Israelites. On his way to curse the Israelites, Balaam's donkey sees an angel blocking the road and refuses to move forward. The author of 2 Peter notes the donkey becomes the one to condemn Balaam for accepting payment in return for casting a curse on the Israelites. In the story, an angel tells Balaam the donkey saved his life (see Numbers 22:22–35).

The author uses images from nature to describe the aridness of these false prophets. He says they are like waterless springs, mists driven by the wind, who inherit the gloom of darkness. They use their high-sounding talk to lure others back to the paganism from which they freed themselves. Playing on the passions and lustful desires of others, the false prophets promise freedom while they themselves are slaves to their own corruption. Just as slaves belong under the control of their masters, so those who allow themselves to be controlled by anything become a slave to that thing.

The author of 2 Peter declares anyone who broke from the slavery of sin through the knowledge of the Lord and Savior Jesus Christ and then falls back into this slavery is worse than one who never converted. He writes it would have been better not to learn the way of righteousness than to learn it, only to leave it. He applies a message from Proverbs to describe the terrible condition of those who learned about Christ and turned away. Proverbs states: "As dogs return to their vomit, so fools repeat their folly" (Proverbs 26:11). To return to the slavery of sin after learning about Christ is as repulsive as a dog returning to his vomit, or the newly washed pig returning to wallow in the mud.

Review Questions

1. What does the author of 2 Peter say about the need for abundant knowledge and virtue?
2. Why does the author feel the need to continually remind his listeners of truths they already believe? What does that mean for our life?
3. What does the author mean when he says no prophecy of Scripture is a matter of personal interpretation?
4. What were some of the teachings of the false teachers?
5. What examples from past history does the author use to convince his readers to remain faithful to the Lord?
6. Why does the author feel a need to warn his readers not to fall away after having learned the truth about Jesus Christ?

Closing Prayer (SEE PAGE 16)

Pray the closing prayer now or after *lectio divina.*

Lectio Divina (SEE PAGE 9)

Relax your body and maintain a posture of prayer (back straight, eyes shut, feet flat on the floor). This exercise can take as long as you want, but in the context of this Bible study, 10 to 20 minutes should be sufficient.

The meditations that follow are provided only to help group participants use this prayer form, but note that *lectio* is intended to bring one to a place of prayerful contemplation where the Word of God speaks to the hearer from his or her heart. (See page 9 for further instruction.)

Living With Spiritual Knowledge (1:1–11)

A nun was teaching a group of adults about Christ when a woman raised her hand and said, "Sister, just teach us to love Jesus. We don't need all the things you are teaching about his life." The nun explained that true love and spirituality are not built on devotion alone, but on true knowledge about Jesus and his message. She added that many false devotional practices had their source in a false teaching about Jesus. Saints like Teresa of Ávila believed strongly in the need to base her devotion on a true knowledge of Jesus' life and message.

The author of 2 Peter recognizes the importance of true knowledge when he prays that readers should experience peace through knowledge of God and Jesus Christ. He urges his readers to supplement their faith through the practice of virtue based on true knowledge. Christians, who spend time reading and learning more about the Church and Scriptures, base their spirituality on a true knowledge of God and Jesus. True knowledge of the Scriptures can lead to the practice of true virtue.

✠ *What can I learn from this passage?*

Apostolic Witness (1:12–21)

On the day of Jesus' resurrection, he appeared to his disciples, and Thomas, one of the Twelve, was not with them. When they informed Thomas that Jesus had been raised from the dead, Thomas refused to believe it, saying unless his put his finger into the nail marks and his hand into Jesus' side, he would not believe. A week later, Jesus again appeared to his disciples, and Thomas was with them. Jesus told Thomas to put his finger into his nail marks and his hand into his side. When Thomas saw Jesus, he expressed his belief that Jesus had truly been raised, proclaiming, "My Lord and my God!" (John 20:28). Jesus said in response, "Blessed are those who have not seen and have believed" (John 20:29).

Christians today have not seen the resurrected Christ, but billions throughout the world believe he has been raised. We believe because we have faith through the power of the Holy Spirit. The author of 2 Peter declares no prophecy in Scripture ever came because a human being desired it, but it was spoken through the power of the Holy Spirit. When we believe in the resurrection of Jesus without seeing it, our faith comes to us as a gift of the Holy Spirit. Faith is believing what we do not see. With faith, we can proclaim with Thomas, "My Lord and my God."

✠ *What can I learn from this passage?*

False Teachers (2)

King Saul, chosen by God to be the first king of Israel, was a noble and religious man when he became king, totally dedicated to the one true God of Israel. In time, however, he began to worship other false gods, so God took the kingship away from the offspring of Saul and his family. The Lord chose David as the second king of Israel. Although David sinned, he never abandoned the one true God of Israel to worship false idols. In the days of Saul and David, many people in Israel worshiped the God of the Israelites, but they also worshiped other idols. The struggle for many was to realize the God of the Israelites was the one and only true God, and other gods did not exist.

Many Christians worship the one true God, yet Christians encounter many of the daily temptations of life that could lure them away from remaining faithful to the Lord. The false gods many may worship could be the gods of greed or illicit pleasure. These temptations can become the center of their endeavors in life and they can forget to make the Lord central to their life. Faithful Christians are those who live in the midst of the world without allowing the enticements of a worldly life become their false gods. Many people who were once close to the Lord have abandoned their faith in God and rejected the Lord for the goods of the world. We live in a society that applauds visible success, but one that often overlooks the need for spiritual success which is not seen with the eye. The author of 2 Peter warns against following the false prophets of society.

✠ *What can I learn from this passage?*

PART 2: INDIVIDUAL STUDY (2 PETER 3)

Day 1: The Coming Day of the Lord (2 Peter 3:1–10)

The author speaks of this letter as being the second one sent to these readers. He is probably alluding to 1 Peter, although this cannot be held as proof that both letters were written by the same author. An anonymous author, writing in Peter's name, would make his letter sound more authentic by linking it with a previous letter attributed to Peter.

The author of 2 Peter tells his readers he is writing to them for the same reason found in his first letter, namely, they might have a correct understanding of the words of the prophets and the message of Jesus, the Lord and Savior. The importance of the apostolic tradition is shown as the author recalls they have received this message of Jesus through the apostles.

The letter challenges the thinking of those who are denying that the world will come to an end and that God is active in creation. In reminding his readers of the words of the apostles, the author recalls that a prediction of the last days foretold by false prophets would arise, such as those now among them. Their presence is proof the final days have come. The early apostles foretold these prophets would be a scornful, self-seeking group who would mock the promises concerning the last days. The author of 2 Peter is aware he is writing two generations or more after Jesus was on earth, and some of his readers, who are growing impatient waiting for the end times, are willing to listen to these false prophets.

The false prophets are asking when this Second Coming, or *parousia*, will occur, saying everything is the same as it was during the time of their ancestors. These ancestors may refer to the prophets of the Old Testament or to the early apostles of Christianity. The false prophets declare nothing has changed since their ancestors fell asleep, which was their way of saying that their loved ones had died. Not only has the world gone on since the time of their ancestors, but also it remains as it was since the beginning of creation.

The author of 2 Peter responds by reminding his readers the heavens and earth were formed in the midst of the waters that covered the earth. This was brought about by the Word of God, and the same Word of God destroyed the world by means of the Flood. The Word of God has now destined the heavens and earth to be destroyed by fire on the Day of Judgment, when "the godless" will be destroyed.

The author continues to speak of the Second Coming of Christ as something that will take place despite the teachings of the false prophets. He reminds his readers of an Old Testament psalm that states God views time differently than we do. With God, a day is like a thousand years, and a thousand years like a day (see Psalm 90:4). Although, in our view, Christ is slow in coming, in reality the Lord is patient with us so no one will be lost and all people will have a change of heart. The delay, which is a result of the Lord's patience, will end at some point in time, and the day of the Lord will come as unexpectedly as a thief. On that day, the heavens will vanish with a roar, the elements will be dissolved by fire, and the earth and all its deeds will be disclosed.

Lectio Divina

Spend 8 to 10 minutes in silent contemplation of the following passage:

Since we live more than 2,000 years after the birth of Jesus, some self-proclaimed critics scoff at Christians who believe some day the world will end with the coming of Christ. History brought us a large number of evangelical preachers who predicted a time for the world to end, but it never happened. According to Jesus, no one knows when the world will end (see Mark 13:32). We could imagine people many centuries in the future saying, "Five thousand years ago, when Jesus was born...." According to 2 Peter and Paul the Apostle, it is the loving patience of God that keeps the world in existence. God wants to give everyone a chance for salvation. The longer a sinner lives, the greater the opportunity for a change of life. Only God knows when the world will end. We should live each day as though it were our last.

A certain fact of life is that life will end for all of us, either through our own death or when the world ends.

✠ *What can I learn from this passage?*

Day 2: Being Prepared for the End (3:11–18)

Since everything will come to an end unexpectedly, the author tells his readers they should live holy and godly lives, awaiting and hastening the day of the Lord when the heavens and elements will dissolve and melt away in fire. According to the promise given by Christ, however, there will be new heavens and a new earth where the righteousness of God will reside. Isaiah the prophet speaks of God creating new heavens and a new earth in which the former things shall not be remembered (see Isaiah 65:17). The new righteousness will be so complete that remembrance of evil days will no longer exist. The occurrence of the new heavens and new earth will take place after the final judgment has passed.

The author ends by urging his readers to remain holy and pure and to be at peace in the Lord's sight while they await the Second Coming. Instead of thinking the delay of the Second Coming is a sign of God's lack of activity in the world, they should view it as a sign of the Lord's patient concern for the salvation of all people. In the eyes of the Lord, a thousand years are like a day. The reason for the delay in the Lord's Second Coming is God's patient desire that all people will have time for repentance.

The author refers to Paul, whom he calls a beloved brother (a fellow Christian and apostle). In his letters, Paul informed his audience about these mysteries of the Second Coming of Christ, but some were ignorant and unstable, finding Paul's message hard to understand. In his Letter to the Romans, Paul refers to the patience of God by asking if his readers hold the Lord's "patience in low esteem, unaware that the kindness of God would lead you to repentance" (Romans 2:4). Those who lack faith distort Paul's message as they distort the rest of the Scriptures, and they cause their own destruction. The reference to Paul suggests some members of the Church at the end of the first century already viewed Paul's letters as having equal authority with the Hebrew Scriptures.

The author notes those who read his letter are now forewarned. They are to avoid losing the security of their beliefs that will happen if they accept the errors of the wicked. As the author of 2 Peter has done at the beginning of this letter, he stresses the need for true knowledge, praying his readers will increase in grace and the knowledge of Jesus Christ, the Lord and Savior. It is this true knowledge of Jesus Christ that is being challenged by the false prophets denounced in this letter. The letter ends with a prayer of praise for Christ, both now and forever.

Lectio Divina

Spend 8 to 10 minutes in silent contemplation of the following passage?

Living a virtuous life to be prepared for the end that will come as unexpectedly as a thief in the night is important, but we also have a mission to perform on earth with the time God gives us. Looking for the end of the world is a useless endeavor since it will end for us one way or another. In the meantime, God wants us to live a holy life and fulfill our mission on earth. Be prepared for the end by doing well what we are called to do now.

In a parable, Jesus compares the end to a man who travels abroad and leaves his servants in charge, each with their own work. The man will return some day when the servants least expect him. The hope is when the master returns, he will not find the servants sleeping. Jesus' sums up the end of time with one word of advice: "Watch" (Mark 13:37).

A man had a friend whom he knew had a daily routine of praying for fifteen minutes in the morning before going to work and then working as hard as he could throughout the rest of the day. Before supper, the friend would spend a short time praying, eat his meal with his family, and spend the rest of the evening watching television with his wife and children. The man asked his friend what he would do differently if he knew this was to be the last day of his life. His friend said, "I would live that last day in the same way I now live each day." He was prepared.

✠ *What can I learn from this passage?*

Review Questions

1. Why does the author of 2 Peter feel a need to warn against those who scoff at the Second Coming of Christ?

2. What reason does the author give for God's delay of the Second Coming of Christ?

3. What does the author of 2 Peter tell us about a new heaven and a new earth?

4. What advice does 2 Peter give concerning preparation for the end times?

Living as Children of God

1 JOHN 1—5

Beloved, we are God's children now; what we shall be has not yet been revealed. We do know that when it is revealed, we shall be like him, for we shall see him as he is (3:2).

Opening Prayer (SEE PAGE 16)

Context

Part 1: 1 John 1—3:10 Most commentators believe 1 John clearly belongs to the school of Johannine Christianity due to its similarity in terminology and concepts found in the Gospel of John. Its development of themes, similar to those of the fourth Gospel, shows the author wrote the letter after the fourth Gospel was written, placing the date of its composition around the end of the first century. It does not begin with the customary greeting and identification of the author, nor does it end with the usual salutation found in most letters. It can be classified as a theological treatise that stresses theological themes not found in other New Testament letters.

Despite its similarities with the Gospel of John, 1 John appears to have been written by another author due to its differences in style and some concepts used. Commentators date the letter as having been written no earlier than the year 100.

Although he does not identify himself, the unknown author begins the letter writing as though he were John and a witness to Christ. He claims he not only heard the Lord's message and saw the Lord, but he also touched him. The message of the Lord concerns the Word of life that he will now share with his readers so they may have eternal life with those who were with the Lord. God is light, and those who walk in light have unity with the Son of God, Jesus, who takes away all sins. He reminds his readers of the commandment of love that they already received. Addressing all members of the community, he tells them not to love the world or the things of the world, reminding them many antichrists have already appeared in the world. He urges his readers to remain faithful to Christ, grateful for his coming. The world will not know the children of God because they did not know Christ. He urges his readers to live a holy life so God may remain in them.

Part 2: 1 John 3:11—5 The author urges his readers to love one another, using Christ who laid down his life for us as an example of the love they should show to one another. In the midst of many false prophets, they will encounter many false spiritual occurrences, but they should test them by their acknowledgment of Jesus Christ who came among them. Those who belong to God listen to God. The author urges his readers to love one another because love is of God, and those who love are begotten by God and know God. Love is this, not that we have loved God, but that God loved us and sent his only Son. God is love, and those who remain in God remain in love. The author tells his readers that with this love and faith they will be victors in the world. He ends with a prayer for sinners.

PART 1: GROUP STUDY (1 JOHN 1—3:10)

Read aloud 1 John 1—3:10.

1:1–4 The Word of Life

The opening line of 1 John speaks of that which was "from the beginning." The Gospel of John begins with a similar idea, stating, "In the beginning was the Word" (John 1:1). John's Gospel, however, was alluding to the preexistence of the Word, whereas this letter refers to the beginning when the disciples first encountered Jesus. In this case, the beginning refers to the time when the author first heard, saw, and came in touch with the message and person of Jesus Christ. He is speaking of his own beginning experiences of Jesus.

The author preaches about the historical Jesus, the Word of life, who became visible and whose life the author claims to have witnessed. Although he does not refer to the preexistence of the Word of life, he does proclaim that Jesus Christ shared in eternal life with the Father, an eternal life that became visible in Jesus, who was the Word become flesh who "made his dwelling among us" (John 1:14).

What the author has heard and seen, he proclaims to the reader so the reader may be in union with him (the author) whose communion is with the Father and with the Son, Jesus Christ. Just as the Father and the Son are one, so the author, by being in union with Jesus, is also in union with the Father and the Son. Since the letter was written around the turn of the first century, the author was most likely not an actual eyewitness to the presence of Jesus Christ on earth. As one belonging to the Johannine community, however, he can declare he shares this witness in common with the community, a witness that had its origin with those who knew Jesus and lived with him. He knows that John, who was one of the Twelve, walked with Jesus. He declares he finds joy in sharing this message with them.

1:5–10 God Is Light

In the Gospel of John, the author often contrasts light with darkness, informing us Jesus is the Light of the World, and "the light shines in the darkness" (John 1:5). In 1 John, the author refers to God as "light" (1:5), and tells us no darkness resides in God. Those who claim to have unity with God while they walk in the darkness of evil ways are liars in word and deed. The author identifies darkness with those choosing to live sinful lives. Those who walk in the light not only live in unity with God but also in unity with one another. Walking in light refers to walking in truth and holiness. The author states it is the cross and resurrection, that is, the blood of Jesus Christ, that cleanses us from the darkness of sin.

Instead of denying we are guilty when we sin, we should trust God to forgive us when we admit our sinfulness. If we choose to deny our sinfulness when we are in sin, then we are choosing to live in darkness. We are deceiving ourselves and avoiding the truth. When we acknowledge our sins, the true and just God will cleanse us from all sinfulness, thus turning our darkness into light.

When we deny our sinfulness, we deny the revelation given by God through the Scriptures, thereby making a liar out of God. We thus drive God's Word out of our lives, leading us to shun God's forgiveness.

2:1–11 A New Commandment of Love

The author uses the expression "my children" in addressing his audience, a common scriptural reference to the followers of Jesus. At the Last Supper, Jesus addresses his disciples as "children," and tells them he will be with them "only a little while longer" (John 13:33). After the resurrection, Jesus appears to his disciples standing on a shore while they are fishing, and he shouts out to them, "Children, have you caught anything to eat?" (John 21:5). Paul uses the expression in his First Letter to the Corinthians: "I am writing to you not to shame you, but to admonish you as my beloved children" (1 Corinthians 4:14).

The author of 1 John states he is writing to keep them from sin, yet, if they do sin, they should remember they have an Advocate (Jesus Christ) before the Father. In the Gospel of John, Jesus speaks of sending an Advocate to his disciples, but he does not refer to himself as the Advocate, but to "the Spirit of truth" (John 14:17), which commentators view as a reference to the Holy Spirit. Jesus Christ, as the Advocate in this passage, is the "righteous one" (2:1). Jesus comes as an offering for sins, not only for those who believe but also for all people of the world.

According to the author of 1 John, true knowledge of Christ is not simply knowing about Christ but living the commandments established by Christ. Those who claim to know Christ without living his message are liars, and they lack the truth specified by Christ. Those who live in accordance with the message of Christ are people of truth and love. Whoever lives the commandments as established by Christ can be assured they are living "in union with him" (2:5).

The author of 1 John informs his readers he is not giving them a new commandment but an old commandment they had from the beginning, meaning they learned it when they first had faith in Christ. In another sense, however, it is a new commandment. In living this commandment, the Christian makes it new as he or she personally relates to God in love. When a person acts in union with the risen Christ, light overcomes darkness. To claim to love God, who is light, and to hate one's brother or sister leaves a person living in darkness. The one who loves one's neighbor is living in the light, and thus has no fear of stumbling. The opposite is true of the one who hates a brother or sister and walks in the darkness. Blinded by the darkness, such a person has no idea where he or she is going.

2:12–17 Remaining Faithful

In this passage, the author addresses "children," "fathers," and "young men." Commentators are divided over the meaning of these titles. Some claim they refer to those who are new in the faith (children), old in the faith (fathers), or those maturing in the faith (young people). Others claim they are references to different offices within the Church. The author addresses each group once and then addresses them a second time.

In his first address to the children, he writes to them because they have had their sins forgiven in Christ's name. In his first address to the fathers, he writes because they have known the Father who is from the beginning, that is, eternal. In his first address to the young people, he writes because they are strong in faith, living God's Word and overcoming the evil one.

In his second address to the children, he writes because they truly know the Father. In his second address to the fathers, he repeats what he wrote to them in his first address. He writes to them because they know the Father who is from the beginning. In his second address to the young people, he writes because they remain strong and the Word of God lives on in them. He repeats they have conquered the evil one.

The author warns his readers against loving the world or the things of the world. In speaking of loving the world, the author is referring to all that is opposed to God. Those who love the world leave no room for the Father's love, since the desires of the flesh, namely sensual lust, temptations for the eyes, and a conceited life do not come from God but from the world. The world and its evil desires will pass away, while those who are faithful to the will of God will live forever. Although Christians must live in the world, they must fight against the allurements of self-gratification found in the world.

2:18–29 Antichrists

The author of 1 John declares this is the last hour. In the early Church community, the last hour not only indicated the last days, but it also indicated the time when the power of evil would make its last strong effort to turn the people away from God. This power of evil will come as the antichrist, that is, an individual or group of antichrists who will stand in opposition to Christ. The author tells his readers they once heard the antichrist (the power of evil) was coming, and now they are witnessing the many antichrists that have appeared. Unlike opponents outside of Christianity (such as the religious leaders who challenged Jesus in the Gospel stories), the opponents of Christ are now found within the community. The letter writer warns his audience against these false Christians.

The author states these evil people left the community, adding they never really belonged. If they belonged to the community, they would have remained. They proved they never belonged, since they would not have left if they did.

Anointing was considered a symbol of strength, and Christians were anointed in the sacrament of baptism. The spiritual strength, which came to them through their anointing, also gave them knowledge and enabled them to live the faith. The author writes to remind his audience they are living in true knowledge gained through this anointing from God. The antichrists are those living without truth. They are liars who deny Jesus is the Christ, and in denying the Son, they deny the Father as well. In John's Gospel, we read that the one who rejects the Son also rejects the Father, and the one who accepts the Son also accepts the Father (see John 14:9).

The author urges his readers to remain faithful to the teaching they have learned from the beginning so they will remain in union with the Son and the Father. Those who remain faithful receive the promise of eternal life. The author notes the warnings in his letter are directed toward those who try to deceive themselves. He is not addressing the conduct of those who remain faithful. Since they have received knowledge through the anointing and they retain this knowledge, they have no need to learn any new doctrines contrary to that which they have learned. They should follow the teachings that come with this anointing, keeping free from any living lie and remaining faithful to Christ.

The author of 1 John again addresses his readers as children, reminding them to remain faithful to the Lord so they may confidently greet him and not have to be shamed by him at his coming. The imagery of hiding their shame recalls the sin of Adam and Eve as described in Genesis. After they sinned, they hid from God in shame, knowing they had sinned and were naked (see Genesis 3:8–10). Since God is righteous, then everyone who remains faithful and lives a just life is a child of God, begotten by the Lord.

3:1–10 Those Who Belong to God

The author of 1 John speaks about the love the Father has bestowed on us in allowing us to be called children of God. This gift of being a child of God came to us through the Son. In the Gospel of John, we read: "But to those who did accept him (Jesus) he gave power to become children of God..." (John 1:12). Although we are indeed children of God, the world does not understand what the call to be a child of God means. In speaking of the world, the author is speaking of those attuned only to the material world that has no idea about the spiritual realm of life. These people judge only by what they see with their eyes. The reason the world does not know the followers of Christ is because the world did not know Jesus. Jesus said, "If the world hates you, realize that it hated me first" (John 15:18). Many of the people of Jesus' era saw him only as a human, with no idea about his divinity.

The author of 1 John teaches that Christians now share as children of God, and in the age to come, when all becomes light, Christians will be like Jesus Christ. At that time, they will see Christ as he truly exists. Those who hope in Christ make themselves pure, as Christ is pure.

Opposed to those who live in the purity of the risen Christ are those who live in sin, which the author identifies as "lawlessness." Just as the author of the letter contrasted light and darkness, he now contrasts righteousness and sin. The author warns the "children" (Christians) against deception, stating simply that those who act with righteousness are righteous, just as Jesus is righteous. The person who sins is not a child of God but belongs to the devil. The person who sins is sinful, just as the devil is sinful. The author, saying the devil has been sinful since the beginning, is apparently referring to the first sins recorded in the Scriptures.

The way to determine who is born of God and who is born of the devil is to examine the extent of their love (born of God) or the extent of their sinfulness (born of the devil). The one born of God will share in the holy nature of God, while the one born of the devil will share in the sinful nature of the devil. The Son of God was revealed to destroy the works of the devil. "God's seed" remains in the righteous, and they are unable to sin since they are begotten of God, which means they have turned their life over to faith in the Lord. The distinction between the children of God and those of the devil is thus clearly revealed. The one who does not act with righteousness or who does not love brother or sister is a child of the devil.

Review Questions

1. What does the author of 1 John say about his witness to the Lord?
2. What constitutes light and darkness in the eyes of the author of 1 John?
3. How can we be sure we know God?
4. What is the new commandment the author of 1 John teaches?
5. Who are the antichrists?
6. What does the author say about God's anointing?
7. How are we to live as children of God?

Closing Prayer (SEE PAGE 16)

Pray the closing prayer now or after *lectio divina*.

Lectio Divina (SEE PAGE 9)

Relax your body and maintain a posture of prayer (back straight, eyes shut, feet flat on the floor). This exercise can take as long as you want, but in the context of this Bible study, 10 to 20 minutes should be sufficient.

The meditations that follow are provided only to help group participants use this prayer form, but note that *lectio* is intended to bring one to a place of prayerful contemplation where the Word of God speaks to the hearer from his or her heart. (See page 9 for further instruction.)

The Word of Life (1:1–4)

A man saw an elderly woman standing by a stranded car on a highway one winter evening. She was elegantly dressed and clearly distraught about her predicament. She had a flat tire. Despite the freezing weather, the man proceeded to change her tire for her. When he finished, she handed him a hundred-dollar bill. He tried to refuse it, but she insisted, saying that she could afford it. Then she said, "If you don't want to keep it, pass it on."

The man stopped at a diner for a steaming bowl of soup and a hot cup of coffee. The woman waiting on him was neatly dressed but obviously poor. He noticed that her shoes were worn and the small jacket she wore was almost threadbare. When he finished, he gave her the hundred-dollar bill as a tip. At first, she refused to take it, but he insisted and said to her, "If you don't want it, pass it on."

That night, on her way home from work, the woman stopped at her mother's house. "Mom," she said, "a man gave me a hundred-dollar bill, and I want you to use it to buy the medicine you need." The mother tried to refuse, but the girl insisted. When the mother asked what she could do in return, the girl told her about the man and how he told her to "pass it on." She said to her mother, "Buy your medicine. Who knows, some day you may be able to help someone else in some way and pass on some goodness."

The author of 1 John is passing on valuable information. He speaks of being a witness of the Lord, and he knows he has the duty of passing on the goodness he experienced. Knowing and loving Jesus has led many holy men and women to joyfully pass on the good news of Jesus Christ. What the author received, he is now passing on to others.

✠ *What can I learn from this passage?*

God Is Light (1:5–10)

There is an old fable of the sun lighting up the day and the darkness in a cave suddenly being able to communicate, even though they were far apart from each other. Since light had never seen darkness and darkness had never seen light, they decided to exchange places so they could see what the other saw. Darkness came out into the light and shouted in amazement at the dazzling brightness. The sun then went into the dark cave, but the cave could no longer remain dark in the presence of the sun. Darkness suddenly realized that wherever the sunlight went, darkness could not exist. It would be impossible for sunlight not to overcome the darkness.

The author of 1 John tells us that God is light. Where God is, a person's faith can be warm, bright, and joyful. Those who live close to the Lord are living in the light of Christ and can experience the love and peace of Christ in their hearts. The light of Christ always overcomes the darkness of sin in the world. When we live in sin, we are living in darkness, shutting out the light who is God.

✠ *What can I learn from this passage?*

A New Commandment of Love (2:1–11)

Someone once said, "What you do shouts so loudly that I can't hear what you're saying." Another expression declares, "Actions speak louder than words." The author of 2 John is telling us we can claim to be a follower of Christ, but unless we reflect the love of Christ through our actions, we are, in effect, lying. If we say we love God and do not show love to a brother or sister, we are living a lie. If we claim to be a true reflection of Christ's love when we refuse to love a brother or sister, we are acting as though God is a liar, since we believe we are faithfully reflecting Christ. To reflect Christ, we must learn to love our brothers and sisters in the world.

✠ *What can I learn from this passage?*

Remaining Faithful (2:12–17)

A spiritual writer once wrote we should strive to practice the presence of God in our daily life. Although we live in the world with all its cares, worries, and temptations, we believe God is with us in our struggles. In reality, it is impossible to think of God every moment of the day and at the same time give our attention to performing the tasks God has given to us in our state of life. Human beings have wandering minds. Even as we pray, we may forget about God and become distracted by our daily needs or concerns.

Many people who pray the rosary complain they can be at the second or third decade and realize they were not paying attention to their prayer but were thinking of the day ahead. Spiritual writers tell us never to go back and repeat the decades. God knows human nature and knows we have wandering minds. We do our best and may fail. To want to pray is to pray.

Practicing the presence of God is a prayer. We practice the presence of God even when we are not thinking of God. It is an attitude of mind. Just as a married man or woman do not think of each other every moment of the day, they have a consciousness of each other that influences many of their actions throughout the day. Because they are married, there are actions they can and cannot perform. They think as married people.

Our attitude of mind should be toward loving God, a love that has an influence on many of our actions during the day. When we develop this attitude of mind, we are practicing the presence of God. In doing this, we are following the direction of the author of 1 John, who urges us to love God more than the things of this world.

✠ *What can I learn from this passage?*

Antichrists (2:18–29)

During Jesus' passion, he endured great physical and emotional pain. His physical pain is obvious, but his emotional pain is often overlooked. During his public ministry, Jesus showed great concern for his twelve closest companions, eating with them, teaching them, and berating them when necessary. The betrayal of Jesus by Judas, one of the Twelve, must have pained Jesus deeply. Judas may have eaten at Jesus' house with the other apostles, and Jesus' Mother Mary may have served him. At the time of Jesus' passion, Jesus' friend, Judas, not only left his company but he also led soldiers to the Mount of Olives to capture Jesus. Knowing the soldiers may not recognize Jesus, Judas gave them a signal, saying the one he kisses is Jesus. When Judas kissed Jesus, Jesus asks sadly, "Judas, are you betraying the Son of Man with a kiss?" (Luke 22:48). This betrayal by a friend was an added affliction to Jesus' agony in the Garden.

The author of 1 John writes that the antichrists came from among those who once claimed to be one of them, a follower of the message given by Jesus. He says they never really belonged to Christ because they never fully understood the truth about him. Judas never fully understood the truth about Jesus, and he became the first antichrist in betraying Jesus. The author of 1 John warns us there may be some who identify themselves as Christians while attempting to teach others a distortion of the truth about Jesus. What we learn about Jesus should be tested against Jesus' message found in the Scriptures.

✠ *What can I learn from this passage?*

Those Who Belong to God (3:1–10)

Pope Francis said that all Christians receive the call to holiness. He noted that the holy people are the saints of every day, the hidden saints, practicing a sort of middle-class holiness.

The saints had one goal in mind, namely to remain loyal to God, no matter what happened in their lives. They were single-minded when it came to following Jesus. They endured temptation, pain, doubt, rejection, and death for Christ. Many people think of the saints as men and women who had no difficulties in following Jesus. They picture the saints as always conscious of God's presence in their lives. The reality is saints had to struggle with their faith as we do. If they had such a great grace in their life that they could never have to endure the struggles of being human, then they would not be saints. Saints merit sainthood because they were as human as we are and endured all that our human nature must endure. It is safe to say that those recognized as saints by the Church never thought of themselves as worthy of being called saints.

We are all called to be saints, which means we are all called to be single-minded in following Jesus. The author of 1 John tells us we have the seed of God within us, which means we can become saints with the guidance, help, and protection of the Holy Spirit. Following the advice of Pope Francis, we can all become middle-class saints by performing our daily tasks with love of God and neighbor (see his homily of April 14, 2013). In referring to this "middle class of holiness," he simply means we are saints who live normal lives, loving God as best as we can. Love is the centerpiece of holiness.

✠ *What can I learn from this passage?*

PART 2: INDIVIDUAL STUDY (1 JOHN 3:11—5)

Day 1: Love One Another (3:11–24)

The author reminds his audience they were taught to love one another from the first time they heard the message of Jesus Christ preached to them. He uses Cain (who killed his brother, Abel) as an example of one "who belonged to the evil one" (3:12). Because Cain was evil, he hated the deeds of the good and killed his brother, whose acts were righteous. The followers of Jesus should not be surprised that the world, which loves evil, hates them.

The followers of Christ have passed from the death of evil ways to life in Christ because of their love for one another. Love for one another was a continual message preached by Jesus. Those who hate their brothers and sisters abide in death, living in the darkness of evil. In reality, they are murderers, and eternal life has no place in the lives of murderers. Jesus gave the ultimate example of love by laying down his life for us. In the same way, we must lay down our life for our brothers and sisters.

The author of 1 John wonders how God's love could possibly survive in the heart of a person who, having been blessed with the resources of this world, refuses to help a brother or sister in need. He tells us love does not consist merely in words, but in deeds and in truth, that is, in belonging to God and acting accordingly. Our words and our manner of acting proclaim our faith.

Even if our hearts should condemn us, we should realize God is greater than our hearts. As long as we are living in peace with God, we are committed to the truth, and that is what matters. The author seems to imply that we are to commit ourselves to the truth, whatever our feelings may be telling us. As long as our conscience does not condemn us, we can stand openly before the Lord and realize we will receive whatever we ask from the Lord.

In keeping the commandments given by Jesus, we will have the security of knowing the Lord rewards those who keep the commandments. The commandments given by Jesus direct us to believe in the Son, Jesus Christ, and to love one another. Believing in the Son presumes we will fulfill whatever the Son asks of us. It is a belief that shows itself in action. Those who keep these commandments live in Christ and Christ in them. This indwelling of Christ includes the indwelling of the Father who is one with Christ. The Spirit we have received enables us to know of God's presence within us.

Lectio Divina

Spend 8 to 10 minutes in silent contemplation of the following passage:

The author of 1 John touches upon a problem that exists for many, namely a person's feeling he or she is not a holy person. Although nearly 2,000 years have passed since the author wrote his letter, the problem people have about feeling holy still remains. The author of the letter reminds us as long as we keep the commandment of love of God and neighbor, we are holy.

Jesus delivered a parable about Judgment Day in which he spoke of separating the sheep from the goats (see Matthew 25:31–46). He invites the sheep, who represent loving people, to share in his glory because they fed him when he was hungry, gave him drink when he was thirsty, welcomed him when he was a stranger, clothed him when he was naked, cared for him when he was ill, and visited him when he was in prison. When those justified ask when did those deeds, he answers that whatever they did for the least of his brothers and sisters, they did for him. The goats represent those who did none of these loving deeds, and they are plunged into eternal fire. What they did not do for others, they did not do for him.

Love of God and love of neighbor involve concern for all people, even those we do not know. We love God and neighbor by praying to God and praying for the good of our neighbor. Performing good deeds for our neighbors, helping them with their needs, bringing peace into their lives, and not causing them unnecessary pain are some of the ways we show love for our neighbor. Prayer and good works make us holy, whether or not we feel holy. Striving to reach out to God and neighbor is God's will for us and the path to holiness.

✠ *What can I learn from this passage?*

Day 2: God Is Love (4)

The author of 1 John is concerned with the Christian's need to distinguish between the true Spirit of God and the false spirits of the world. He states there are many false prophets in the world. He urges his readers not to accept every spirit, but to put the spirits to a test, and he gives them guidelines for this test. The Spirit that acknowledges that Jesus Christ came in the flesh is the Spirit of God. The spirit that does not acknowledge Jesus Christ does not belong to God and is the spirit of the antichrist whose coming was foretold and is already in the world. In 1 Corinthians, Paul teaches about discerning good and bad spirits when he writes, "I tell you that nobody speaking by the spirit of God says, 'Jesus be accursed.' And no one can say, 'Jesus is Lord,' except by the holy Spirit" (1 Corinthians 12:3).

The author of 1 John tells his readers they have conquered the false prophets because God, the one who is greater than the spirit of the world, dwells in them. The false prophets belong to the world and speak the language of the world. Because they belong to the world, the world listens to them. Those who belong to God, however, speak to those who acknowledge God and not to the world, since they do not speak the language of the world. In short, this is the way to discern the truthful Spirit from the deceitful spirit.

Because love has its source in God, we, who are called to love God, are also called to love one another. Those who live in this love are born of God and have a living knowledge of God. Those who lack this love do not know God, because God is love. When God sent his Son into the world so that we could share eternal life with him, God's love was revealed to us. In the Gospel of John, we read: "For God so loved the world that he gave his only Son, so that everyone who believes in him might not perish but might have eternal life" (John 3:16).

The revelation concerning God's love is beyond our expectations. The truth of God's love is not that we love God, but that God first loved us and sent his Son into the world as an offering for our sins. If God shows such love for us, then we must love God and one another.

The author states "no one has ever seen God" (4:12). He does not include Jesus Christ in this statement. In the Gospel of John, we read, "No one has ever seen God. The only Son, God, who is at the Father's side, has revealed him" (John 1:18). Although we have never seen God, God dwells in us when we love one another, and, in loving one another, God's love is active within us, being perfected in us. Love becomes perfected in us when we put God's love into action in our life.

Through the gift of God's Spirit, we know we remain one with God and God remains with us. The author declares that by the power of the Spirit, we see and witness the Father who sent the Son as Savior of the world. We see through the eyes of faith and, through faith and the gift of the Spirit, we witness to the love of God. When we testify Jesus is the Son of God, God remains in us and we in God.

The author of 1 John continues by stating not only that God has love but also that God *is* love. In an earlier part of the letter, the author told us God is light; he now adds God is love. Because God is love, we live in this love as we live in God. If we love with God's love, then we should have no fear on the Day of Judgment, since we are living with God's attitude toward the world, which is love. We fear judgment because we have fear of punishment, but love overcomes the fear of punishment. The one who fears is not yet perfect in love. We are able to love because God first loved us.

The author reminds us that the love of God should be a model for our love. To claim to love God and, at the same time, refuse to love a neighbor, amounts to living a lie. People cannot love God, whom they do not see, and hate their neighbor, whom they do see. In summary, this is God's commandment: Those who love God must also love their brothers and sisters. In John's Gospel we read: "As I have loved you, so you also should love one another" (John 13:34).

Lectio Divina

Spend 8 to 10 minutes in silent contemplation of the following passage:

When the cardinals elected Jorge Mario Bergoglio Pope on March 13, 2013, he established the direction of his papacy immediately by choosing the name Francis in recognition of the poverty of St. Francis of Assisi. In the days after his election, Pope Francis showed himself to be a humble servant of all people by choosing as simple a lifestyle as he could for a pontiff. He also exuded a great deal of humility and love for all people. In doing this, he was not only following the example of Francis, but he was also recognizing that his ministry is one of reflecting the love of God for all people.

The author of 1 John informs us that we do not say God has love, but that God *is* love. That means anytime we show true love for others as Jesus, St. Francis of Assisi, or Pope Francis did, we are sharing in the love of God. Since God is love, every action of true, selfless love, is an action of God in the world. God is love, and we are the ones chosen to bring that love to the world.

✠ *What can I learn from this passage?*

Day 3: The Spirit, Water, and Blood (5)

Those who have faith in Jesus Christ are born of God, and those who love the Father also love the one begotten of God. When we love God and live according to God's commands, we are also living with love for those begotten by God, that is, the children of God. We show our love for God by keeping God's commandments. Jesus said, "If you love me, you will keep my commandments" (John 14:15). The commands of God are not a burden for those who love. When we keep the commandments of the Lord, we show we are begotten of God (God's children) and can conquer the world. The author of 1 John exclaims that the one who believes Jesus is the Son of God and acts accordingly is the one who is victor over the world. The love of Christ is more powerful than all the weapons of the world.

Jesus came to us through water and blood, that is, through his baptism and his crucifixion. The Spirit is a witness to this, and the Spirit is truth. In the Gospel of John, we read John the Baptist testified about Jesus saying, "I saw the Spirit come down like a dove from the sky and remain upon him" (John 1:32). The author of 1 John claims we now have three witnesses: the Spirit, water, and blood. Jesus told his disciples, "When the Advocate comes whom I will send you from the Father...he will testify to me" (John 15:26).

The testimony given by God is now far greater than any human testimony. Those who live with faith in the Son of God have accepted this testimony, while those who do not believe have rejected the message of God, thus making God a liar. The testimony given by God is the message that God has given eternal life to those who have faith in the Son of God. Those who have this faith have eternal life, while those who disbelieve do not possess eternal life.

The author of 2 John tells his readers he has written these words so those who have faith in the name of the Son of God, that is, faith in the Son of God, will know they possess eternal life. The author calls us to trust in prayer. He tells us that as we are praying, we can be confident God is answering our prayer. In Matthew's Gospel, Jesus declared, "Ask and it will be given to you; seek and you will find; knock and the door will be opened to you" (Matthew 7:7).

We must keep in mind this passage concerning prayer written by the author of 1 John is speaking about living in faith and acting in love. True prayer should be based on these two motives. Those who see a brother or sister in sin should pray for that brother or sister. Through this prayer, life will be given to him or her, providing the sin is not deadly. Although the author of 1 John does not identify this deadly sin, some commentators believe he is referring to those sinners who have cut themselves off from the community by denying that the Son of God became flesh in Jesus Christ. Since these false teachings were the occasion for this letter, such a conclusion is logical. The deadly sin could also be a reference to the unforgivable sin by which a person rejects the promptings of the Holy Spirit. In Mark's Gospel, we read, "Whoever blasphemes against the holy Spirit will never have forgiveness, but is guilty of an everlasting sin" (Mark 3:29). When a person rejects God's graces, he or she puts up a wall against God's blessing in his or her life.

The author of 1 John states that the one born of God cannot sin, because God protects him or her from evil. Those who have chosen to follow the ways of the world are under the influence of the evil one, while those who have chosen to follow God are free of sin. The Son of God came to help us know the one true God and to teach us life in the Son is also life in the Father. The Son is true God, and, as God, is eternal life.

The author of 1 John concludes with a warning that his readers should avoid all idols. The false idols include all false teachings that lead a person away from God. This refers to those who teach the Son of God did not become flesh in Jesus Christ.

Lectio Divina

Spend 8 to 10 minutes in silent contemplation of the following passage:

A second-century martyr named Polycarp lived a long life and, at the age of eighty-six, was ordered to offer incense to the emperor as an act of religious homage. The people of his era believed the emperor was a god, and refusal to offer incense indicated a person was an atheist. Polycarp refused to offer incense. In the face of death, he asked how anyone could expect him to deny the Lord and Savior whom he served for eighty-six years. He told his persecutors to bring on whatever they wished. He was burned at the stake for his faith.

Saint Polycarp lived in an era when the people considered anyone who would not worship the Roman gods to be an atheist. They accused Polycarp of being an atheist, but it is reported that when he neared death, he pointed to the people around him and courageously accused them of being true atheists. He remained firm in his faith of the one true God.

The author of 1 John wanted to be sure that Christians to whom he was writing would remain firm in their faith. Like Polycarp, many of them would be challenged to accept false teachings and worship the idols of the day. The author of 1 John encourages them to remain firm in their faith, aware that those who believe in Christ will merit eternal life.

✠ *What can I learn from this passage?*

Review Questions

1. What does the author mean when he says everyone who hates his brother is a murderer?
2. What must Christians do to have confidence that they are not condemned by God?
3. How can Christians test the Spirit?
4. What does the author say about God and love?
5. Why is it important for us to love our brothers and sisters?
6. How does our faith help us to have victory over worldliness?

A Message for Salvation

2 JOHN

3 JOHN

JUDE

But you, beloved, build yourselves up in your most holy faith; pray in the holy Spirit. Keep yourselves in the love of God and wait for the mercy of our Lord Jesus Christ that leads to eternal life (Jude v. 20–21).

Opening Prayer (SEE PAGE 16)

Context

Part 1: 2 John The short letters of 2 John and 3 John center on the theme of truth, which refers to true faith in Jesus Christ as the Son of God. Both letters appear to be written by the same author. In each letter, the author identifies himself as "the Presbyter," and they contain similarities in vocabulary and style. In using the simple identification of the Presbyter, the author appears to accept that he is well known to the communities to which he is writing. Many similarities in theme, such as the emphasis on truth and love show a connection with the Gospel of John and 1 John. Commentators believe the letters have their source in the Johannine community.

The author of 2 John urges his readers, whom he addresses as children, to follow the law of truth and love by loving one another and avoiding the doctrines of false teachers.

Part 2: 3 John and Jude In 3 John, the author urges a Christian named Gaius to welcome messengers sent to him to preach about Jesus. The name Gaius may be an unknown individual, or a name used to designate general communities to which the letter is addressed. The author warns about the deceitfulness and ambition of a man named Diotrephes who teaches errors and hinders those seeking the truth. He encourages his readers to do good, since good works belong to God.

Jude contains only twenty-five verses. A similarity in content and style exists between Jude verses 4–16 and 2 Peter 2:1–18. Since it appears unlikely they both had the same common source, then one must have copied from the other. Although Jude appears last among the Universal Letters, many commentators believe it was written before 2 Peter.

The author of this short letter urges his readers to stand firm against those who teach false doctrines. He uses examples from the Old Testament to show the Lord punishes those who attempt to act against the commands of the Lord. He urges his readers to realize there will always be scoffers, but they must not waver in their faith.

PART 1: GROUP STUDY (2 JOHN)

Read aloud 2 John.

Verses 1–6 Walk in Truth

The letter is written by one who calls himself "the Presbyter." This indicates his office in the community that designates him as a person of authority. Many Scripture commentators believe the author of the letter is the same one who wrote 1 John.

The author addresses his letter to the "chosen Lady," a title that could be used to designate a specific individual, but most likely used in this letter to designate a specific church community. In mentioning that she is chosen, the author is stressing the idea that God is the one who chooses, not the community. The author also addresses the letter to "her children," a further sign it is written to members of that particular church community.

The author expresses his love for this church and expresses the love of others who hold truth in common with her, a truth that is eternal. The truth refers to those who live with faith in Jesus Christ in opposition to false teachings. In union with this truth and love, all share in the grace, mercy, and peace that come from God the Father and from Jesus Christ, the Father's Son. This reference to Jesus Christ as the Father's Son is the basic message of this letter against those who deny Jesus is the Son of God who came in the flesh. The books of the Johannine community stress the messages of truth and the love of God.

Following the customary format used in letter writing, the author follows his greeting with an expression of thanksgiving. The emphasis remains on the idea of the truth, which is faith in Jesus Christ. He rejoices that some of the children of the chosen Lady are waking in truth, which, in Johannine writing, refers to remaining faithful to the truth, as commanded by the Father. When he refers to "some of your children," he may simply be implying he is speaking of the faith of those he encountered and not all the members of the community. He could be viewing those he encountered as representative of the faith of the total community.

The author does not offer a new commandment to his readers, but he urges them to live the commandment of loving one another. In the Gospel of John, we read that Jesus gave a new commandment to his disciples when he said, "I give you a new commandment: love one another. As I have loved you, so you also should love one another" (John 13:34). The author of 2 John is telling his readers they must follow the commandment of love they received from the beginning, that is, from the time they first became Christians.

Verses 7–13 The Need to Remain Faithful

The warnings given in this letter recall the same warnings given in 1 John. Itinerant preachers are leading the people into believing Jesus Christ did not come in the flesh. As he has done in 1 John, the author calls these deceivers "antichrists." He warns the community not to abandon the teachings for which they have worked and which will bring them a full reward.

The Christians being addressed by the author have received their instruction about Jesus, the Son of God, from the first time they entered the faith. Now, a new teaching is being given, one that denies the Son of God became flesh. Those who choose to follow this new teaching will no longer be rooted in the Church, and they will not have God in their lives. Those who remain faithful will continue to possess both the Father and the Son. The author warns his audience to avoid those who bring false teachings into the community. Those who welcome these false teachers will share responsibility for their wicked deeds.

The author concludes by stating he has much to say to them, and he hopes to visit with them soon, rather than write to them. He states this would bring him great joy. He sends greetings from the members of the Johannine community in which the Presbyter is currently living.

Walk in Truth (Verses 1–6)

When Jesus stood before Pilate during his passion, Jesus said to Pilate, "Everyone who belongs to the truth listens to my voice" (John 18:37). Jesus meant that everyone who accepts faith in Jesus Christ and acts accordingly belongs to the truth. Pilate, who was a pagan, asks, "What is truth" (John 18:38). The author of the Gospel of John is telling us that those who do not believe in Jesus as the Son of God can never know real truth, since real truth offers an answer for the whole meaning of creation. Pilate, who does not know Jesus as the Christ, must always seek in vain for the answer to his question, "What is truth?"

The author of 2 John teaches that truth is not something we know, but it is something that takes possession of our total being. He tells us, "the truth that dwells in us....will be with us forever" (1:2). Once we accept the truth that Jesus Christ is the Son of God and make this belief the center of our life, we are living in the truth.

✠ *What can I learn from this passage?*

The Need to Remain Faithful (Verses 7–13)

In Matthew's Gospel, we read the story of the Magi seeking the newborn king of the Jews. They travel to Jerusalem where they ask King Herod for information concerning the newborn king. Herod, disturbed by the news, consults the chief priests and scribes and learns the newborn king was to be born in Bethlehem of Judea. King Herod directs the Magi to go and find this newborn king and bring him news so he may also go and worship the child. The Magi follow the star that leads them to the home where Jesus was. Upon their arrival, they pay homage to the Child and present gifts to him. Later, in a dream, they receive a warning not to return to Herod, so they "departed for their country by another way" (Matthew 2:12).

The author of 2 John speaks of deceivers living among the Christians. These deceivers deny that Jesus, the Son of God, has become human, and they attempt to teach others their false doctrines. The author warns his readers not to lose what they have worked so hard to believe. In a sense, he is saying that when they encounter these deceivers, they should go on with their lives another way, without returning to the falsehoods of their past life. As believers, they are paying homage to Jesus, and they should not allow themselves to be contaminated by deceptive teachings.

When Christians encounter certain worldly ideas that could appear to be so logical, right, and sincere, but which lead away from Christ, they should go home by another way, that is, they should not allow deceptive ideas to lead them to betray Christ.

✠ *What can I learn from this passage?*

Review Questions

1. Why does the author of 2 John urge his readers to follow the command to love one another?
2. What does the author of 2 John mean when he speaks of loving Gaius "in truth?"
3. How should Christians act toward those who teach false doctrines?

Closing Prayer (SEE PAGE 16)

Pray the closing prayer now or after *lectio divina*.

Lectio Divina (SEE PAGE 9)

Relax your body and maintain a posture of prayer (back straight, eyes shut, feet flat on the floor). This exercise can take as long as you want, but in the context of this Bible study, 10 to 20 minutes should be sufficient.

The meditations that follow are provided only to help group participants use this prayer form, but note that *lectio* is intended to bring one to a place of prayerful contemplation where the Word of God speaks to the hearer from his or her heart. (See page 9 for further instruction.)

PART 2: INDIVIDUAL STUDY (3 JOHN AND JUDE)

Day 1: Help in Ministry (3 John)

As in 2 John, 3 John is sent from the Presbyter and is addressed to an unidentified man named Gaius for whom the author expresses his love. All three letters of John appear to be written by the same author. As the author does in 2 John, he writes he loves Gaius "in truth," which means he loves Gaius in his shared faith in Jesus Christ as the Son of God.

The author of 3 John expresses his hope that Gaius is prospering in a healthy manner, just as his soul is prospering, that is, living in God's presence. The news he has heard from some members of his community that Gaius is faithfully living the way of truth brings joy to the heart of the author. Since Gaius was a common name during the New Testament period, the identity of this Gaius is not clear.

The author commends Gaius for showing his faithfulness to the messengers sent by him, even though they were strangers to Gaius. These are the ones who have testified to Gaius' love, and the author urges Gaius to help them—in a spirit pleasing to God—on the remainder of their journey. These men set out to preach the truth, and in doing so they depend on the hospitality of other Christians. They refuse to accept any support from pagans, thus avoiding any accusation they are profiting from pagans. Those who help them share in their good works.

The author states the messengers began their mission "for the sake of the Name," which refers to their mission in the name of Jesus. In the Acts of the Apostles, Luke speaks of the apostles who were imprisoned and freed by the religious rulers in Jerusalem (the Sanhedrin) with a warning not to speak about Jesus Christ again, an order which they rejected. Luke writes, "So they left the presence of the Sanhedrin, rejoicing that they had been found worthy to suffer dishonor for the sake of the name" (Acts 5:41).

Contrasted with Gaius is Diotrephes, one who apparently holds an office of leadership in some manner, but who refuses to accept any messengers from the author of 3 John, perhaps out of personal ambition. The author warns that, if he visits, he will tell everyone about Diotrephes' behavior and the evil accusations he is spreading about the author and his messengers. Diotrephes goes so far as to prevent other members of the community from receiving these messengers, and he expels them from the church if they do so. The refusal of Diotrephes to accept the author and his messengers underlines the need for Gaius to accept them.

The author warns his readers not to follow the example of evil but to follow the example of those who are good. He states the obvious, saying those who are doing what is good are of God, and those who do what is evil have never seen God. Seeing God does not refer to a vision of God, but to faith in God.

The author cites a man named Demetrius, apparently a messenger sent by the author, as an example of one who is good. Everyone testifies favorably about him, and his living of the truth also speaks for him. The author himself adds his testimony to that of others and notes his readers can believe his testimony is true.

As in 2 John, the author states he wishes to write more, but he would rather talk face-to-face, which he hopes to do soon. He ends with the usual greeting of peace and sends greetings from his community to each member of Gaius' community.

Lectio Divina

Spend 8 to 10 minutes in silent contemplation of the following passage:

> Many years ago, two men began a significant project that has touched millions of lives. They began Alcoholics Anonymous, a movement that helped many addicted men and women to live a very successful and profitable life. Many recovering alcoholics become sponsors for other alcoholics, meeting and welcoming them as they struggle for recovery. Not only has AA helped many alcoholics become recovering alcoholics, it also demonstrated the value of one person welcoming and encouraging another.

together in the heavenly places in Christ Jesus, 7 that in the ages to come He might show the exceeding riches of His grace in His kindness toward us in Christ Jesus." There is a physical realm and a spirit realm. Both are present right here and right now.

We should be in the world but not of the world.

2 Corinthians 5:6-8 *"6 So we are always confident, knowing that while we are at home in the body we are absent from the Lord. 7 For we walk by faith, not by sight. 8 We are confident, yes, well pleased rather to be absent from the body and to be present with the Lord."*

August 11, 2024

Sermon Series: Philippians

Philippians 3:17-4:1

"Citizens of Heaven"

Why do I have a responsibility to vote? Why do I have a responsibility to vote for values, like life and liberty? Why do I have a responsibility to vote for women and men who will continue uphold the freedom of religion? Why? Because I am a Citizen of Heaven.

The author of 3 John writes to someone named Gaius. He knew that some of the missionaries going to the area where Gaius lived needed support, and he urged him to help them in a way worthy of God. He recognized the success of their mission would depend on the acceptance and support of those who believed in Jesus as the Son of God. The message for us today is that Christians can support and accept each other in their attempt to live a life worthy of God.

✠ *What can I learn from this passage?*

Day 2: Warning Against False Teachers (Jude)

The author identifies himself as Jude and refers to himself as a slave of Jesus Christ, a common title used by early Christian writers. In Paul's Letter to the Romans, he begins by identifying himself as "Paul, a slave of Christ Jesus" (Romans 1:1). The word "slave" tells of the author's commitment to the service of Christ. The author further identifies himself as a brother of James, but he omits identifying himself as an apostle, which implies he is not the Jude, or Judas, who was one of the Twelve. The names Jude and Judas often referred to a person with the same name. In Matthew, we read of another Jude or Judas when the people of Nazareth identify Jesus as one of their neighbors. They ask about Jesus, "Is not his mother named Mary and his brothers James, Joseph, Simon, and Judas" (Matthew 13:55). Being a "brother" in the Israelite culture could mean a person was related (often a cousin), but not always in the sense of a sibling. This Judas (Jude) could be considered the author of this letter.

The letter is not written to any community in particular, but to Christians in general. The author addresses them as "called, beloved in God the Father and kept safe for Jesus Christ" (1:1). Just as the author is a slave for Jesus Christ, so those addressed are willing slaves safely guarded by Jesus Christ. He wishes his audience the usual mercy, peace, and love that begin many early letters.

The author states he had planned to write to them about salvation that they all share, but some crisis concerning heresies has arisen in their midst, and the author changed his reason for addressing them. He tells his readers that he feels the need to encourage them to fight hard for the faith that was once given to them. Faith in this letter refers to the doctrine they received from the early apostles, a doctrine now being challenged by heretics.

The author declares some people who have infiltrated their ranks as Christians. Christians should not be surprised at this, since they were warned in past writings about such wicked people intruding into their ranks. The author may be referring here to the writings of the early apostles, such as Paul. Those who intrude are the ones who were foretold and already condemned. They deny Jesus Christ, the true Master and Lord of all, and turn the gifts of God into excuses for sinning sexually. This may be a reference to those false teachers who state that sins of the world no longer count, since Christians have been freed from this world by Jesus Christ. They teach that sins of the flesh do not condemn them because Christ freed them from life in the flesh.

Just as the author has recalled for them the faith that they have received once and for all, so he warns them of the punishment that never changes. God has saved people in the past, but their sinfulness was a source of condemnation. Christians who believe they are saved merely by being called Christians must realize they too can fall from grace just as these great figures of the past fell.

The author offers a series of examples of God's wrath on people once favored by God. The people of Israel were saved from Egypt by God, and God destroyed those who later refused to believe the Lord's Word. The angels received a great gift, but the Lord placed those who abandoned their proper position in eternal chains, a prison of darkness until the Day of Judgment. The well-known towns of Sodom and Gomorrah provide an example of sexual promiscuity and unnatural vice, which led God to punish them with eternal fire.

The author refers to "those dreamers," heretics of his own day, and accuses them of deluding themselves by defiling their bodies, rejecting authority, and reviling angelic beings. They are no better than those condemned in the past. The author refers to an ancient (apocryphal) writing called "The Assumption of Moses," which speaks of the Archangel Michael confronting the devil, who tries to steal Moses' corpse. Instead of arguing with the devil, Michael leaves the act of judging to the Lord while he accepts his role of being the messenger or agent of that judgment. The false prophets and heretics of Jude's day lack such sophistication. They slander and revile what they don't understand. The author states they act like "irrational animals" and will bring about their own destruction.

The author of Jude, continuing to name others who were condemned in the past and who stand as examples of deserved punishment, casts a bitter judgment ("woe") on these false teachers and sinners. He names Cain, Balaam, and Korah, three figures from the Old Testament who turned away from God. Cain killed his brother Abel (see Genesis 4:8); Balaam was hired to curse the Israelites, but God would not allow it (see Numbers 21—24); Korah rebelled against Moses and he and his household were swallowed up by the earth (see Numbers 16).

The author of Jude compares Christian heretics to these three punished sinners. He declares these heretics are empty creatures who are like dark stains on the Christian banquet table, referred to by the author as "love feasts," sharing in the Eucharist in a spirit of revelry and selfishness. The author finds examples for their emptiness in nature. He states they are like useless wind-blown clouds that never give rain. He likens them to the barren fruit tree in late autumn that is dead not only because it is barren, but also because it is uprooted. He sees them as the froth on waves, which splash about uselessly. The heretics are also like shooting stars, which will spend eternity in darkness. In the Book of Enoch, an ancient book that is not a part of the Old Testament Scriptures, stars represent angels. Since the author is familiar with the Book of Enoch, he may be speaking of sinful angels in this passage.

The author quotes from Enoch, who was the seventh generation from Adam. The Book of Enoch was not written by him, but was apparently written within the three centuries before Christ. The author chooses a passage from Enoch that speaks of the Lord coming with a large array of his holy ones to judge all people, convicting the godless for every wicked deed they performed and for every harsh word they spoke against him. The author implies the wicked heretics of his age will receive this harsh judgment. Commentators believe Jude's use of the Book of Enoch shows he has a great regard for the book, as many of his own era did, but it was never accepted as one of the books of the Bible. Jude also makes use of another popular writing of his day: an apocryphal account of the burial of Moses.

In the final sentence of this passage, the author lists the vices of these heretics, calling them grumblers and malcontents who follow their own lusts. He adds they are boastful and flatter others for their own advantage.

Many in the early Church who preached in Christ's name gave warnings that false Christians who sought only their own sinful desires would infiltrate Christianity in the last days. The author writes about these warnings so that the faithful Christians will not be shocked at the discovery of such heretics in their midst. Although the author does not name the types of heresies, he tells his readers these false Christians are selfish people who do not follow the Spirit and who are causing division within Christianity.

In contrast to these selfish, false Christians, the author addresses those who are faithful, telling them to continue to build up their faith and to pray in the Holy Spirit. The gift of faith comes from the Spirit, and the Spirit continues to share in the development of this faith. These Christians are urged to remain faithful to the love of God in their lives and to await patiently the mercy of the Lord Jesus Christ that leads to eternal life.

Christians must continue to be concerned for one another. The author urges them to correct those who have doubts and to save those who will listen from destruction. In their compassion, they must still be on their guard against those who will not listen and who would contaminate them.

Although Christians live in the midst of crisis, the author of Jude reminds them that God can save them from falling and present them without blemish, rejoicing in the presence of God's glory. The author ends by praising God, who saves us through Jesus Christ the Lord. He prays that glory, majesty, power, and authority will continue to be given to God forever.

Lectio Divina

Spend 8 to 10 minutes in silent contemplation of the following passage:

A reporter wrote a story in his daily paper about a professor in a post-graduate course who told his students to write the name "Jesus" on a sheet of paper and then stomp on it. According to one report, he wanted them to later analyze how they felt about this activity. One student, a Christian, refused to take part in this exercise. Some of the other students may have felt the same as he did, but they feared the repercussions of disobeying the professor. The Christian student showed himself to be courageous and dedicated to his respect for Christ.

Jesus knew most people of the world would be living in secular societies, with little concern for religious beliefs in many parts of the world. The challenge for Christians is to remain faithful to the teachings of Jesus in a materialistic society. Despite the materialistic challenges surrounding those who seek to worship and respect God, the world can still claim a large number of courageous and dedicated believers who are remaining faithful to the Lord. The author of Jude realized the challenges facing Christians in the world, and he urged them to remain firm in their faith in the midst of these challenges.

✠ *What can I learn from this passage?*

Review Questions

1. What does the author of 3 John mean when he praises those "walking in the truth?"
2. Why does the author of Jude reject Diotrephes?
3. Who is Demetrius?

About the Author

William A. Anderson, DMin, PhD, is a presbyter of the Diocese of Wheeling-Charleston, West Virginia. A director of retreats and parish missions, professor, catechist, spiritual director, and a former pastor, he has written extensively on pastoral, spiritual, and religious subjects. Father Anderson earned his doctor of ministry degree from St. Mary's Seminary & University in Baltimore, and his doctorate in sacred theology from Duquesne University in Pittsburgh.

Printed in the USA
CPSIA information can be obtained
at www.ICGtesting.com
JSHW011039131123
51752JS00006B/23